Enjoy!
Love Lizzie x

Earth Hygge

hygge (pronounced "hue-gah") is a
Danish word used to acknowledge
a special feeling or moment

A Source Book for
Heart-Centred Living

Lizzie Willis

Illustrated by Angela Malone

Little Red Hen Publishing

"Creativity is just connecting things."
Steve Jobs

Foreword

Someone once described me as a creative bee, cross-pollinating between various people and businesses within my local community. I loved this idea (and resonated with those words). Perhaps, as you journey through this book, you will imagine that bee, happily buzzing through life and effortlessly alchemising on the way.

In many ways, this book serves as a kind of 'love letter' to my hometown of Deal and South East Kent, UK.

However, if you are holding this book in a place other than South East Kent: Greetings! May you still find this book the welcome tonic for fellow Earth-dwellers I intended it to be.

I have loosely ordered the various activities to give a sense of seasonal flow ... you may wish to approach this book chronologically or simply dive in to a page you are guided to enjoy in that moment.

The intention of this book is to provide loving nudges toward living a simpler, happier and more mindful existence. It is my wish to gently uplift and nourish you in Mind, Body and Soul.
 I would like to thank Angela Malone for her beautiful illustrations which conjure the moments I envisaged perfectly. Her incredible talent has breathed life into my ideas.

With Love & Gratitude,

Lizzie Willis

THANK YOU

Thank you to the many businesses and organisations who had faith in the project and jumped on board with my passion and creativity, your support is hugely appreciated.

Thank you to my mentor and dear friend, Ken Pickering whose advice and belief in me has shaped my creative life.

Daniel at Beta Books, thanks for your help in bringing this book into physical form and for patiently answering all my questions!

Thank you to each and every one of you who has purchased this book.

Breathe

Welcome. Take a seat. Make yourself comfortable.
Let us start at the beginning.

Gently bring awareness to your breath. Perhaps, lovingly place a hand just above your navel. Uncross your legs and arms. Check your body is open, receptive and evenly aligned.

Take a slow breath in through the nose to the count of five and, then, release out through the mouth to the count of five.
Close your eyes.
Repeat.

Now, we are ready.

Come, take my hand and join me on a magical journey...

Rise & Shine!

"Each morning, we are born again. What we do today is what matters most."
Buddha

Watch the sun rise and revel in the majesty of our very own star.

This is such a simple, yet deeply fulfilling experience that many of us seldom take the time out to enjoy. Find out when the sun rises in your area this time of year and set your alarm accordingly. Afterwards, you could use the 'extra' time to do some yoga or meditation followed by a hearty, healthy breakfast to really set the day off to a positive start.

Make Like A Tree

We all know that having plenty of exercise in our lives is beneficial for our overall health and finding exercise that brings you pleasure is key to maintaining a regular pattern.

Improving your fitness has a multitude of benefits such as aiding sleep, reducing the risk of cancer and heart diseases, strengthening your bones and muscles, combating stress and depression and, of course, controlling your weight. It may even have a positive impact on your sex life!

If you have had a good workout, devouring that delicious cake, pizza or wine can be even more joyful!

After all...life is all about balance.

Elisa Ellis has been working in the fitness industry since 2001 and has gradually cultivated a large following for her own business via her no-nonsense approach and professional style. Elisa delivers a range of classes to suit all abilities. She is an absolute powerhouse of a woman and a total embodiment of 'small but mighty' if ever there was one!

To discover more about Elisa Ellis Fitness, join her group on Facebook today!

Declutter

In the spring, it feels natural to want to declutter and deep clean your living space. The benefits of having less 'stuff' in our lives include a greater sense of freedom, increased focus, the ability to clean your home more easily and swiftly plus you might even make some financial gain.

Attempting to downsize your belongings can be overwhelming, so it is best to focus on one achievable area at a time. Try to discern whether you find an item either useful or beautiful: be ruthless.

Freeing yourself from clutter can also relate to other areas of unfinished business in your life. If you are putting off making an important phone call or fixing a leaky tap, these things contribute to mental clutter which also has a negative impact on our lives.

Set aside some time to unearth items to give to charity, re-gift, sell or dump. Once you make a start, you may well find the process incredibly liberating and cleansing!

Gratitude Attitude

Adopting an attitude of gratitude is so much more than demonstrating good manners and research has uncovered that being grateful is linked to improved health both physically and mentally.

One study reported that keeping a gratitude diary or journal can improve sleep whilst another study linked improved self-esteem to being grateful.

We are able to cultivate gratitude in our lives by taking just a few moments (perhaps either at bedtime or first thing in the morning) to feel thankful.

Once you begin listing all the positive stuff, you will feel gratitude begin to work it's magic.

Wake Up & Smell the Coffee

Having a mindful moment can be as simple as taking your time to enjoy a cup of coffee with consciousness. Head to Hut 55 cafe on Deal beach and recline in a sunny deckchair, listening to the calm rhythms of the sea. Notice the warming sensations coming from the cup in your hand, be aware of the rising steam and breathe in the comforting and familiar deep aroma. As you take your first sip, pay attention to the taste and the creamy texture. Ignore distractions from your devices or the thoughts racing in your mind, and instead keep refocusing your attention on the experience of drinking and indulging in the pleasure of the moment.

www.hut55.co.uk
@hut55deal Instagram

www.garageroasted.co.uk
@garageroasted

Mind Yourself

Mental and physical relaxation is the key. It allows us to let go, and as we do, a new understanding can emerge. Options and choices that are hidden from us, as we struggle with our thoughts and emotions, can enter our awareness as we allow ourselves to relax, deeply.

Guy Scantlebury is a Clinical Hypnotherapist helping people with the changes they wish to make in their lives. If you would like to deal with stress and anxiety, stop smoking, lose weight and gain confidence, then Guy would love to hear from you.

Through Hypnotherapy, unconscious 'learning' can be unlearned and a patient is able to release stuck emotions and change repetitive behaviour. The key to all of this is deep relaxation, creating an enjoyable and refreshing experience.

Deal Hypnotherapy

1 Royal Buildings, The Strand, Walmer, Deal.

Email: guy@dealhypnotherapy.com

Be A Little Red Hen

The Little Red Hen is a classic folktale with a cautionary message: we reap what we sow.

In the story, the Hen approaches a variety of other animals for help and they each, in turn, refuse.

The Hen is undeterred and continues her work of planting grains, cutting wheat, grinding flour and baking it into bread.

By the end of the story, the animals were prepared to eat the bread which the Little Red Hen has created completely independently by this point.

However, she refuses their offer of 'help' to eat the bread and enjoys it all herself!

The moral of this story is that there are times in life when help is not always at hand. Circumstances ask us to 'dig deep' and go it alone.

If you want something done right, do it yourself.

Others cannot always see the beauty and value of your creative vision until you show it to them.

The Time is NOW

"Real generosity toward the future lies in giving all to the present."
Albert Camus

Take time to exist in the present moment where you are truly alive.

Liberate yourself from the worries of tomorrow or the pain of the past.

For many of us, this is a case of 'easier said than done'. We WANT to live in the present but our over-stimulated minds find it a struggle.

One simple technique is to practice regular mindfulness tools such as focusing on the 'here and now' and shifting focus away from past and future.

You can easily do this by spending time focusing on your breathing and savouring moments such as eating a piece of delicious chocolate or listening to the rhythm of the waves crashing on the shore. Your senses come in handy here!

Really experience each moment as if you have all the time in the world and nowhere else to be.

Phone a Friend

So many of us rely heavily on social media and text messages to communicate nowadays.

It is no secret that this can lead to carefully curated public lives which bear little resemblance to our true inner experience. This airbrushed version of life can keep friendships in the shallow end and people at arm's length.

Take time to speak to friends in person. Hearing their voice will aid communication on a far deeper level and provide that personal touch we seem to have mislaid in our hectic lives.

Do What You Love

Never has it been so important to prioritise your own wellbeing, which in turn impacts the planet in a positive way. How you do that is totally up to you, but a good suggestion is to get out in the fresh air on little adventures. Perhaps you would prefer to get lost in your favourite book or movie.

Don't get roped into doing your household chores, unless you love doing them – in which case, crack on and enjoy!

Life is short – do what you love.

Purpledaisy Ltd is an eco-friendly housekeeping and cleaning service in Deal, Kent. The friendly team pride themselves on customer satisfaction and an environmentally conscious approach.

www.purpledaisy.co.uk
Follow on Instagram and Facebook!

Open your Windows

In recent times, the advantages of opening your windows often have been highlighted.

When we open our windows, we let fresh air circulate and allow pollutants in the air to escape.

During spring & summer, there is a simple pleasure to be had in opening several windows and feeling the air flow and the warm sunshine pour in.

However, opening the windows can be something we do all year round to maintain the circulation of air and decrease indoor pollutants (such as cleaning products, paints or chemical air fresheners) from our living environment.

Go ahead – throw open those windows!

(Don't) Go Compare!

"Don't compare your life to others. There's no comparison between the sun and the moon. They shine when it's their time."
Unknown

In a world populated by social media addicts, life can seem to be one huge competition if you let it!

Regularly remind yourself that what you are being exposed to from others is likely to be a highly edited, filtered and polished 'best bits' version.

Life would be extremely dull if we all had the same values, tastes and lifestyle. The diverse landscape of opinions, attitudes and behaviours is what allows us to engage with passion and helps inform our own choices.

Yes. That grass may look greener. It's probably Astroturf.

Green Light

"We don't have to engage in grand heroic actions to participate in change. Small acts, when multiplied by millions of people, can transform the world."
Howard Zim

We can all 'do our bit' when it comes to reducing single-use plastic. Suggestions from Greenpeace include adopting the use of re-usable water bottles and coffee cups in addition to ditching the use of plastic straws.

Carrying a canvas tote bag with you is a great way to keep stylish and help the planet too!

Your Little Green Shop is a Deal business for plastic-free living and refill groceries; creating a place where local people within the community can have the opportunity to have a lesser impact on the environment. The aim is to provide customers with the freshest and most delicious ingredients without all the unnecessary plastic packaging.

Your Little Green Shop is currently operating from The Village Community Market, Deal.

Stop by to have a taste!

www.yourlittlegreenshop.com

Follow on Instagram!

You Do You

"Be a first-rate version of yourself, instead of a second-rate version of somebody else."
Judy Garland

Some people seem better at this than others and perhaps it does take a little gumption!

Many of us develop the self-confidence to revel in our true nature as we embrace the aging process and abandon any care of what others may think!

A totally inspirational woman is Iris Apfel (if you are not sure who she is: look her up, she's awesome!) who is an example of someone who has really nailed who they are in this lifetime.

Take time to regularly check in with your own core values and beliefs … are you fully aligned with them? What changes can you make? Is your heart and soul pulling you in a different direction? Are you wearing clothes you feel represent YOU? Are your friends people who deeply resonate with YOU? Are you passionate and inspired in your work? Do you love the items filling up the corners of your home?

Making several changes that you feel could disrupt the sleepy equilibrium of your life is a daunting prospect but living a life you have personally designed is totally worth it!

Get Sh*t Done!

"One day you will wake up and there won't be any more time to do the things you've always wanted. Do it now."
Paulo Coelho

Get organised. Get productive.

As much as it is good for your soul to rest, meditate and accept. It can be equally nourishing for your soul to get it done.

If you have always wanted to do something such as see the twinkling lights of Paris from the Eiffel Tower at dusk, jump out of an aeroplane or write a book. Do it! You are the only person who can make it happen!

JUST DO IT.

Your soul will thank you...

Tree Hugger

Walking and simply 'being' amongst trees is a beautiful and healing experience.

It has been said that hugging a tree (much like hugging anyone else) increases levels of oxytocin which is the hormone responsible for emotional bonding and feelings of calm. Serotonin and dopamine are also released when you give a tree a big squeeze, making you feel happier. Wrapping your arms around the trunk can ignite a reconnection with the natural world and provide a feeling of comfort and relaxation!

Apparently, the term 'tree hugger' was first coined in 1730 when 294 men and 69 women of a branch of Hinduism physically clung to or 'hugged' the trees in their village in order to prevent them from being used to build a palace. Sadly, the phrase 'tree hugger' has frequently been used in a negative way by those who dismiss the importance of protecting the earth and it's vital resources. Here, in this book, it has been adopted as a Badge of Honour for all who appreciate the natural world.

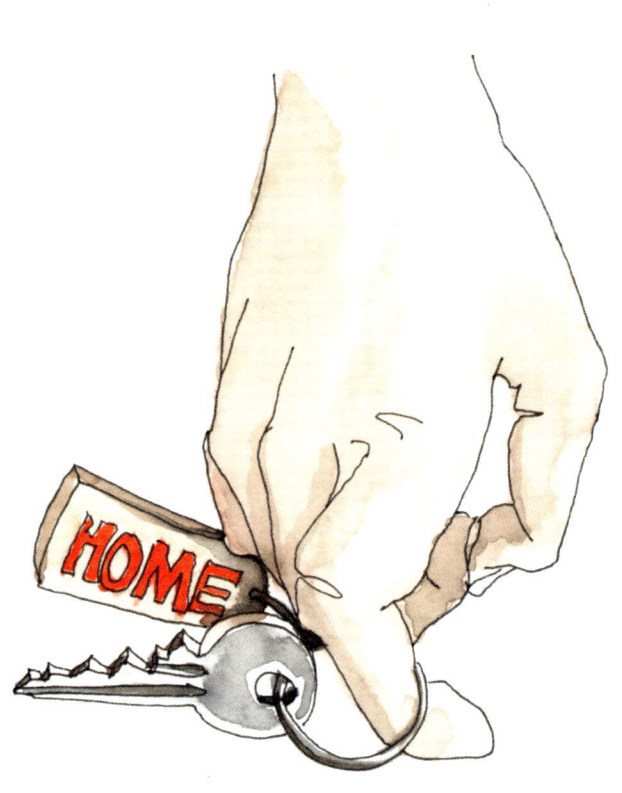

You Hold The Keys

Remember that you hold the keys to your own life. Your surroundings greatly influence your state of mind and, if you feel as though you have outgrown your home (either literally or metaphorically) then perhaps it is time to think about changing your space. A fresh start in a new home is such an exciting adventure and gives you an opportunity to re-invent your style and rethink what you really need and desire from your home.

If you are a first time buyer, this is your opportunity to really take root in a community or you may be thinking about raising a family in your new home. Either way, or both, it is a chance to consider what is important to you and how your new home can grow with you.

Jenkinson Estates is proud to be a fully independent Estate Agent for Deal and the surrounding areas. Their business is focused on a strong 'customer for life' ethos via an accurate, honest and reliable service.

If you are considering buying or selling a home, get in touch!

www.jenkinsonestates.co.uk

Tel: 01304 373984.

Lion Heart

"It is better to be a lion for a day than a sheep all your life."
African Proverb

To be lionhearted is to be brave and determined and lions are widely recognised as a symbol of strength, leadership and loyalty.

We all experience fear, but once we discover the tools to overcome or face our fears then our lives will never be the same again.

Approaching life with a lion heart will undoubtedly inspire others and empower you to walk your path with pride.

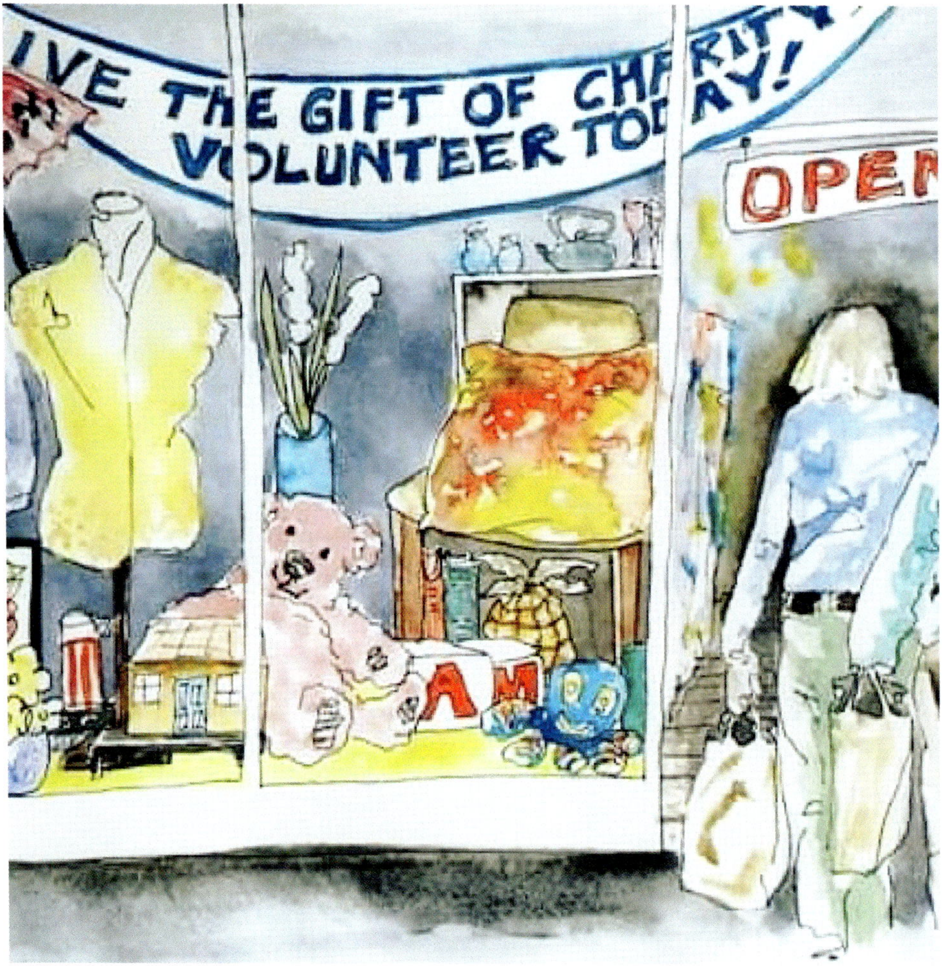
IVE THE GIFT OF CH
VOLUNTEER TO
OPE

Viva Volunteer

If you have the time, consider volunteering.

Gifting your time to volunteer in a charity shop will provide retail skills and experience in addition to meeting new people and contributing to a worthwhile cause.

For the younger generation, it is a useful way of acquiring training and experience - handy for your CV. For the more mature volunteer, it can ease loneliness and depression by providing a sense of purpose and community engagement. It can boost confidence and may help you stay physically and mentally active in your retirement.

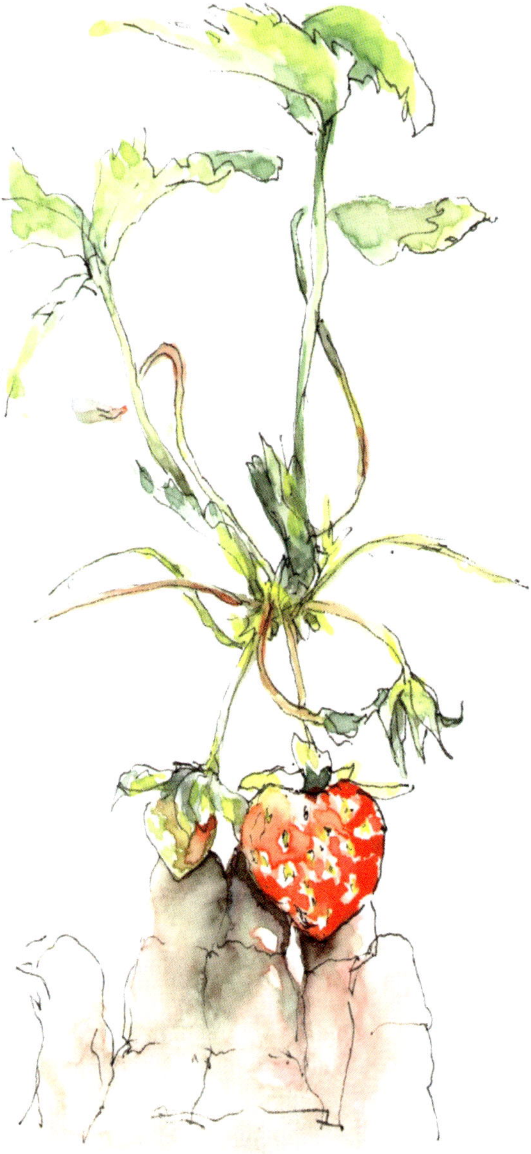

Life is Sweet

It is summer and you are picking strawberries in the warm sunshine.

First, breathe. Take time to notice the detail of the strawberry. Then, you can take a small bite and slowly chew. Close your eyes and swallow.

Strawberries, with their red colour and heart shape, have connotations of passion but also purity and healing. They have been a symbol for Venus, the Goddess of Love and are interestingly a member of the rose family.

No summer picnic or alfresco dining is complete without the addition of strawberries!

Tucked in between the picturesque coastal towns of Sandwich and Deal, Felderland Farm is one of the largest Pick Your Own farms in Kent and grows a wide range of fresh seasonal produce including strawberries!

Felderland Farm has the aim of providing a beautiful setting for an unforgettable day out.

Felderland Farm
Deal Road, Sandwich, CT14 0BJ

FelderlandPYO@bardsley-england.com

www.felderland-pyo.co.uk

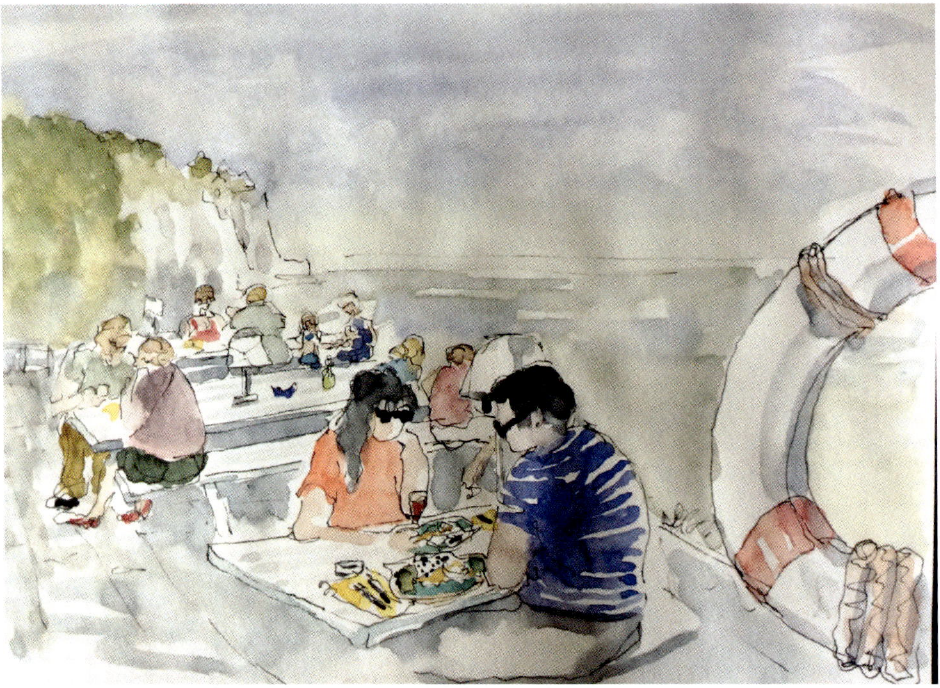

I Do Like To Be Beside The Seaside

Is there a better way to spend a glorious summer day than by the seaside indulging in fish and chips and ice-cream? For centuries, people have visited the seaside for the benefits of taking in fresh sea air and relaxation - escaping the rat race and polluted city air.

The Coastguard is Britain's nearest pub to France and is a gorgeous place to devour fish and chips taking in the stunning views across the Channel. This historic pub situated on the coast of St Margaret's Bay in Kent is a fantastic pit stop to take in Dover's famed White Cliffs and enjoy some delicious, hearty food.

The pub is SO close to France that mobile phones switch their time zones and 'welcome' you to the country - which is always a talking point for amusement with the customers!

In summer, families can explore the nearby rock pools, and in winter the pub is a perfect, romantic and cosy retreat after a bracing coastal walk.

The Coastguard

The Bay, St Margaret's Bay, Dover, Kent

www.thecoastguard.co.uk

Face the Music

We all have issues in our lives we would prefer to brush under the carpet.

Facing the music is about taking a deep breath and tackling those issues we have been avoiding.
This could be a problem in one of your relationships, a niggling worry about your physical health or a financial situation you need to address.

Once you have approached this and found a resolution then give yourself a big pat on the back as you sigh with relief and accomplishment.

See… it wasn't so bad, was it?

Take The Path of Least Resistance

"The path of least resistance is the path that feels best to you."
Abraham Hicks

Sometimes in life, the odds seem stacked against you. When you feel this is starting to happen, go with the flow and accept that perhaps the universe has other plans for you.

It may just be a waste of your valuable life energy to fight against forces out of your control when something even better might be just around the corner.

Get out of your own way and follow the path that feels good.

Then, life usually falls into place.

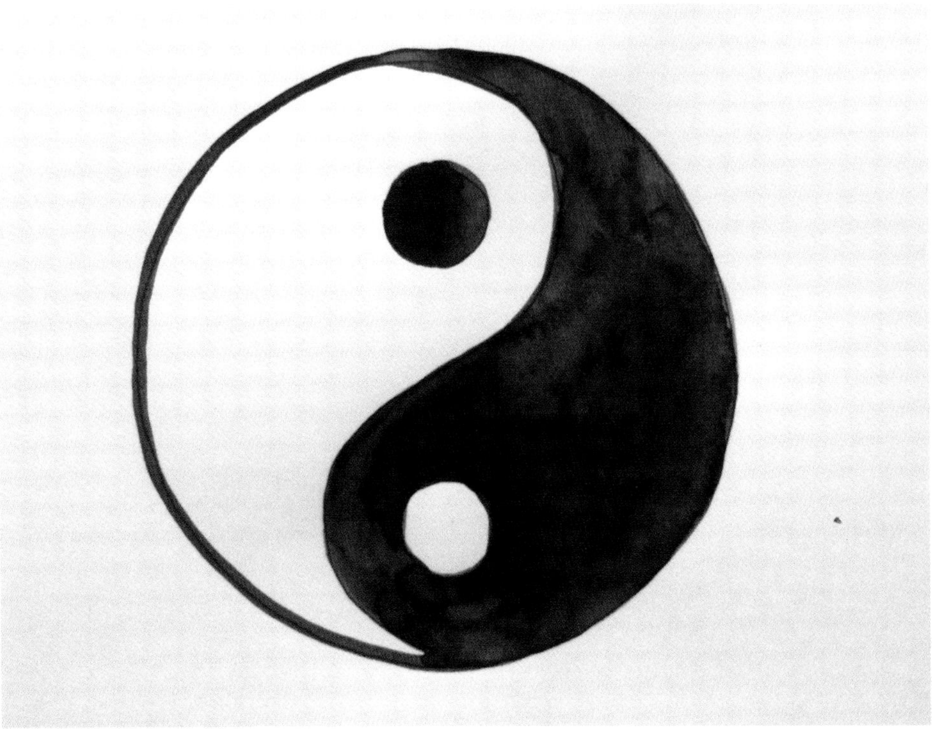

Time for Tai Chi

"Tai Chi is more than a martial art and more than most forms of exercise. It has a deep philosophical and spiritual perspective. Its gentle, slow-motion movements and sophisticated methods of moving life force or chi within the body teach you to relax and open up to your full human potential on all levels – physical, emotional, mental and spiritual."
BK Frantzis

Dave Willis is a qualified B. K. Frantzis Energy Arts instructor and a Registered Instructor with the Tai Chi Union of Great Britain. He has been studying Tai Chi since 2000. He teaches both in Deal and Folkestone, Kent.

The benefits of Tai Chi come about through the deep relaxation of the nervous system and the release of energy blockages rather than through any kind of force. Consequently, it is safe and gentle and can be taken up by virtually anyone.

Sessions include a tea break which helps prevent against the temptation to over strain and allow time for you to absorb the material. It is also a handy time to chat and get to know your class mates. These relaxed and friendly classes are a great way to make friends.

www.taichi.uk.com

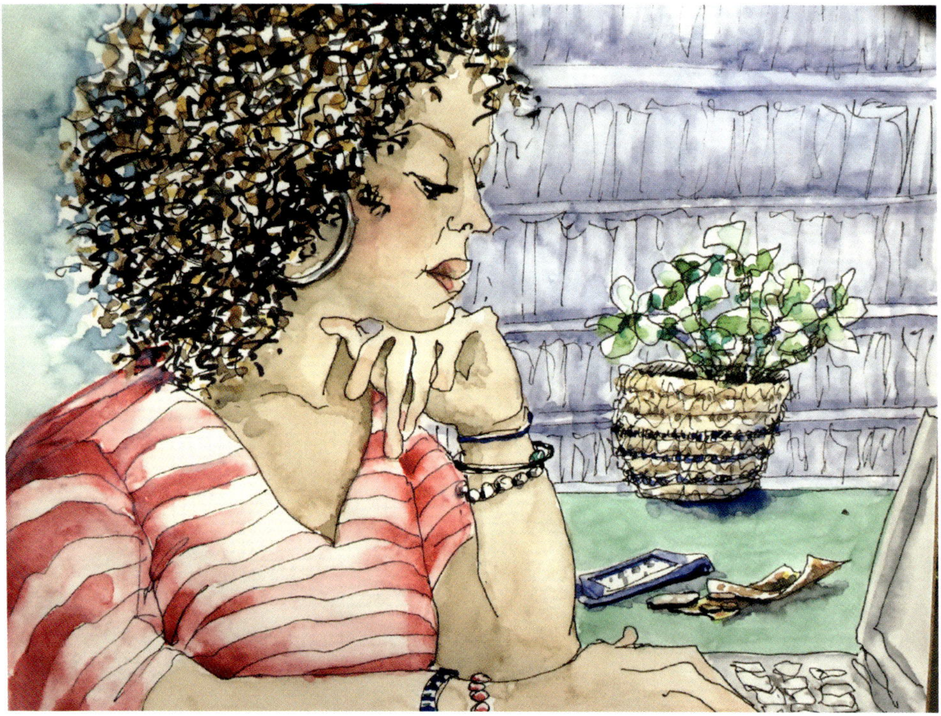

Money, Honey!

One of our most complex relationships in life is our relationship with money.

Financial wellness is an important part of our overall wellbeing and it is vital to have a healthy attitude towards money.

We inherit, or develop, our attitudes towards money in childhood where it can be a seen as a source of both joy but, arguably more often, stress. Attitudes can include feelings of resentment and anxiety resulting in the subject of money becoming a taboo subject in adulthood. Some people get caught up in a competitive Keeping Up With The Joneses cycle or have been conditioned to view money as 'the root of all evil'. These unhealthy attitudes can be addressed and, taking all this into account, it is a wise idea to make an honest and thorough assessment of your finances, perhaps identifying strengths and areas for improvement.

Nowadays, it is common for us to have a 'side hustle' to keep the coffers stacked. If you have launched a small business then it would be a good idea to enlist an expert to help with your accounts and the dreaded annual Tax Return.

The Sandwich Accountancy Group can offer a range of services to assist you with getting on top of your finances and taking out the fear factor in money matters!

Contact Julie today and breathe a sigh of relief that help is at hand!

Email: julie@sandwich-acc.co.uk
148 Dover Road, Sandwich, Kent

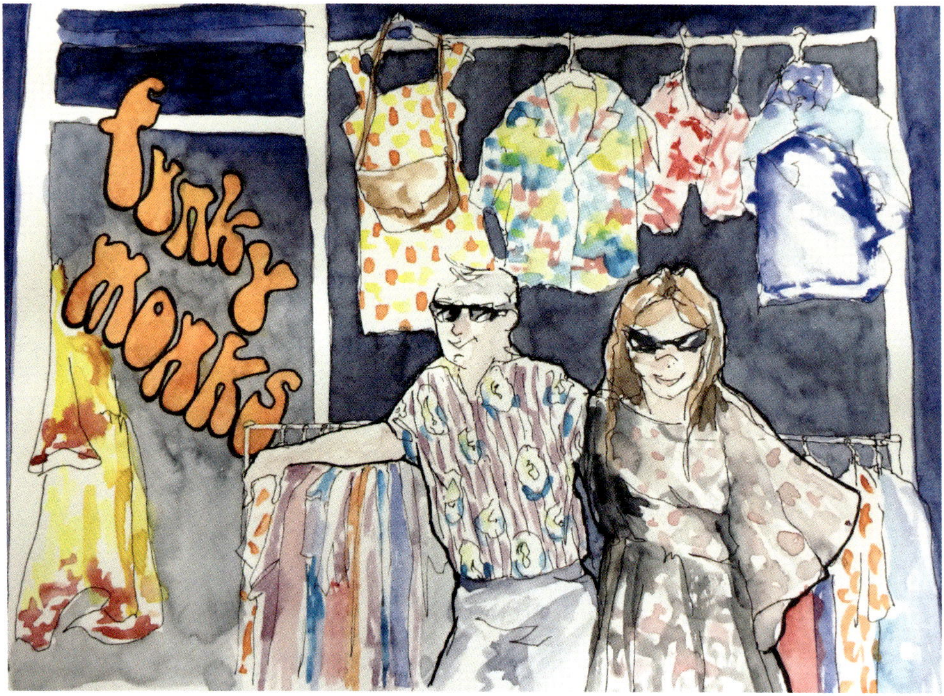
funky monks

Get Funky!

Nowadays, it is more popular than ever to buy vintage and second-hand clothes. Not just because of having something completely unique but because of trying to reduce landfill and helping the planet.

Now, this book is not suggesting it's wrong to buy new garments, but if only people could be more mindful about HOW MANY new items they buy, it would be a great start!

Get thrifting, customise something or start shopping in Vintage and Charity Shops. That way you can still have new regular things rather than constantly buying new and worsening the 'throw away' society that we are now living in.

Brother and sister team, Pete and Kelly both had a passion for clothes and fashion: in the 80s, Pete was into his Punk era whilst Kelly was more into shoulder pads and Stilettos with lightning strikes on the side!

FUNKY MONKS was born in July 1996 and has been a much-loved fixture on Canterbury's St Peter's Street ever since. Customers enjoy having a chat with one of the siblings and returning home with a total one-off purchase.

Follow on Instagram or Facebook.

Embrace Change

"We cannot direct the wind, but we can adjust the sails."

The above quote is attributed to a variety of famous names including Dolly Parton and Jimmy Dean. This gives us a good indication of just how many people these words resonate with.

Life is full of change which is a natural and necessary part of our existence.

Embrace – or at least gracefully accept - life changes as you would the changes of the seasons.

Consider that new opportunities are born out of change and it is a necessary part of life's ebb and flow.

Like Attracts Like

"What you think, you become. What you feel, you attract. What you imagine, you create."
Buddha

Everything in our existence is in a constant state of vibration - objects that seem solid (such as the chair you are sitting on or the table you are eating at) are actually vibrating on different frequencies.

Once you understand this concept, you can start to bend your mind around the idea that 'thoughts become things' and 'like attracts like'. You are the powerful creator of your own reality.

By identifying, thinking about and imagining you have received (or are about to receive) your desires you are using the Universal Law known as The Law of Attraction.

Many people all over the world use these methods to manifest their desires into reality.

This is why it is solid advice to focus on what you want from your life and appreciate the countless positives and expect life to manifest your dreams!

Select – Project – Expect – Collect

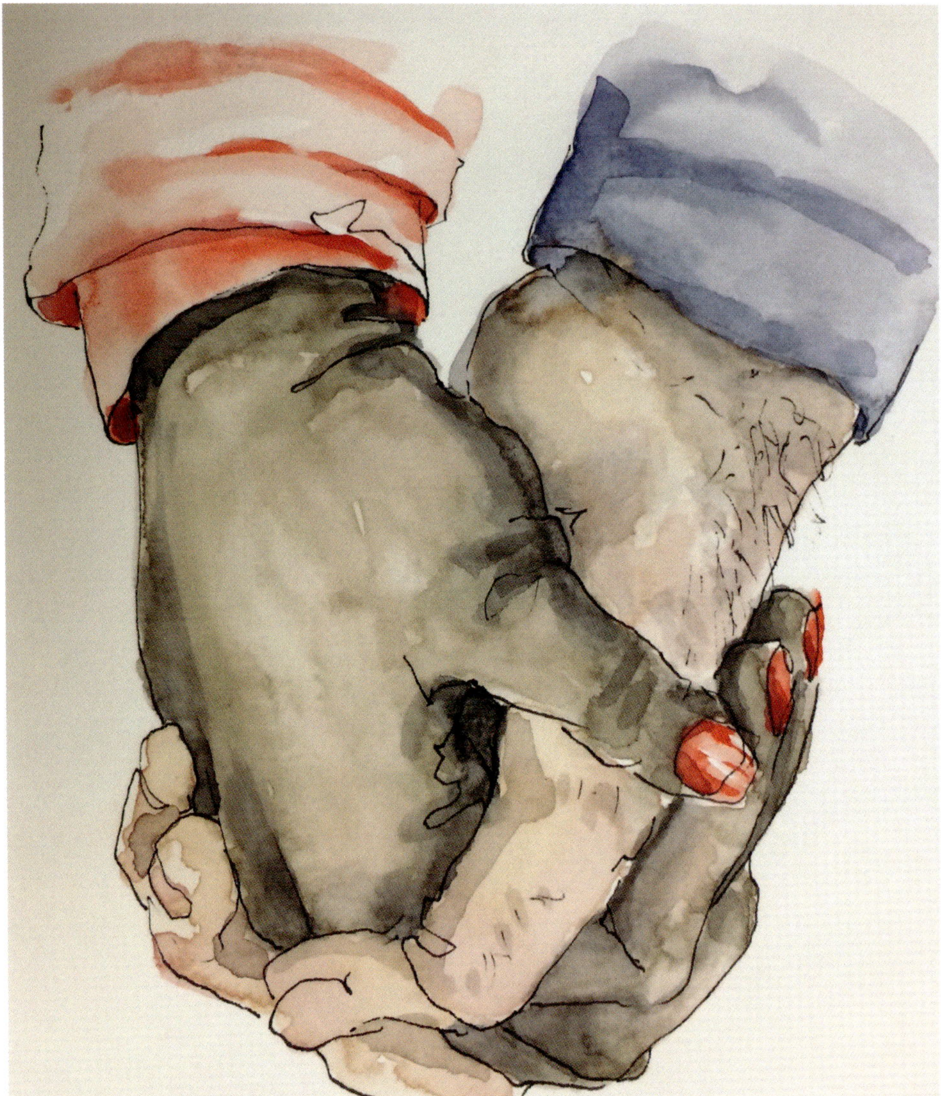

I Wanna Hold Your Hand

Whatever type of relationship you have, there is an intimate connection made when holding hands. Whether you hold hands with your children, best friend or lover, don't be afraid to 'make the first move' and reach out. Enjoy feeling the soothing energy between you both as you connect.

The amazing benefits of holding hands include lower blood pressure, stress hormones and heart rate. Holding hands can boost love, provide security, counteract loneliness and has been reported to reduce pain.

There are times in our lives we may be more likely to hold hands: perhaps in the fuzzy honeymoon of a romance, during the throes of labour (where it could be more of a crush!), holding your toddler's hand as you cross a road or holding the hand of a loved one as they leave their Earthly body behind.

Take my hand...

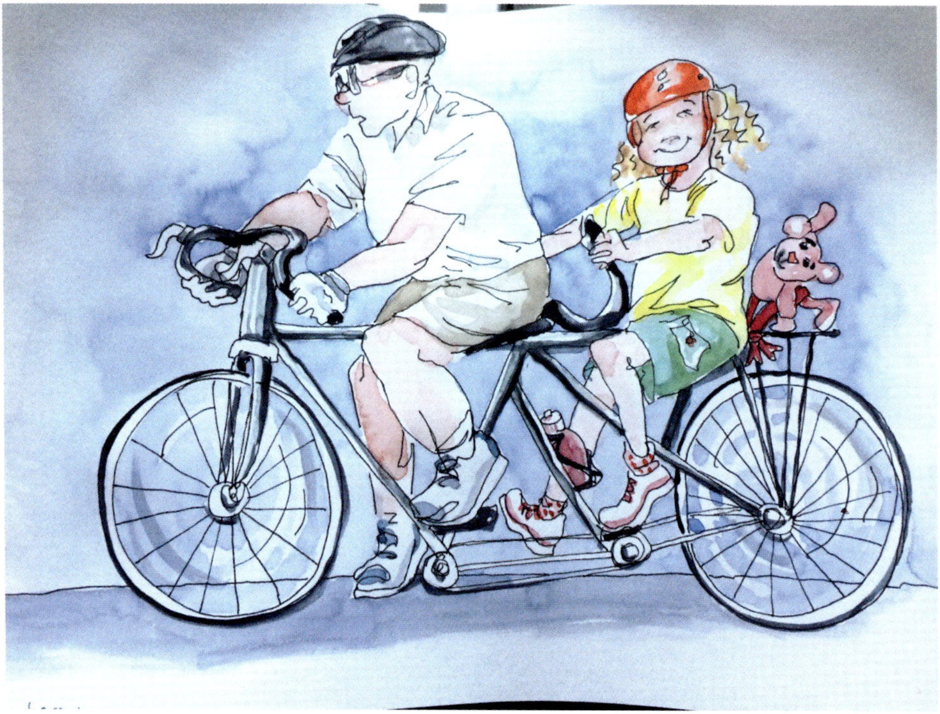

On Yer Bike!

Cycling is a great form of exercise for all the family! Riding a bike is not only fun, but it has a positive impact on your physical body and could help to reduce pollution at the same time. Win win.

Did you know that the world manufactures about 100 million bikes each year?

One of the wonderful things to do in Deal is to cycle along the prom and, lucky for you, you don't even need to have your own bike!

Mike's Bikes is located on the seafront behind Hut 55 (Marine Road, Walmer) and you can hire a range of bikes to suit your needs.

Why not indulge in a 'date day' with someone special by hiring a tandem and providing your own scrumptious picnic?

For further information, check out www.mikesbikesdeal.com.

Cherish Yourself

This is a challenge for many people but try to love yourself more than anyone else!

You could write yourself a love letter full of praise for all the fantastic achievements in your life.

How about looking in the mirror with a sense of adoration and identifying the bits you love.

Carve out time regularly just for you and don't feel guilty about buying yourself gifts.

You are wonderful.

Glass Half Full

"Water is the driving force of all nature."
Leonardo da Vinci

The human body consists of about 60%-70% water so it makes sense that we should frequently hydrate ourselves. The aim is to consume around 6-8 glasses a day but you may require more if you are exercising or if it's a hot day!

Drinking plenty of water has so many health benefits such as reducing sugar cravings, improving memory and mood, preventing headaches, supporting the digestive system, reducing the risk of bladder infections and flushing out toxins.

Fascinating scientific studies have also discovered that water can respond to positive language and thought by creating beautiful crystals (seen under a microscope).

Find a glass and fill it up with purifying, glorious water. Give thanks for everything it does for you on a daily basis.

Bottoms up.

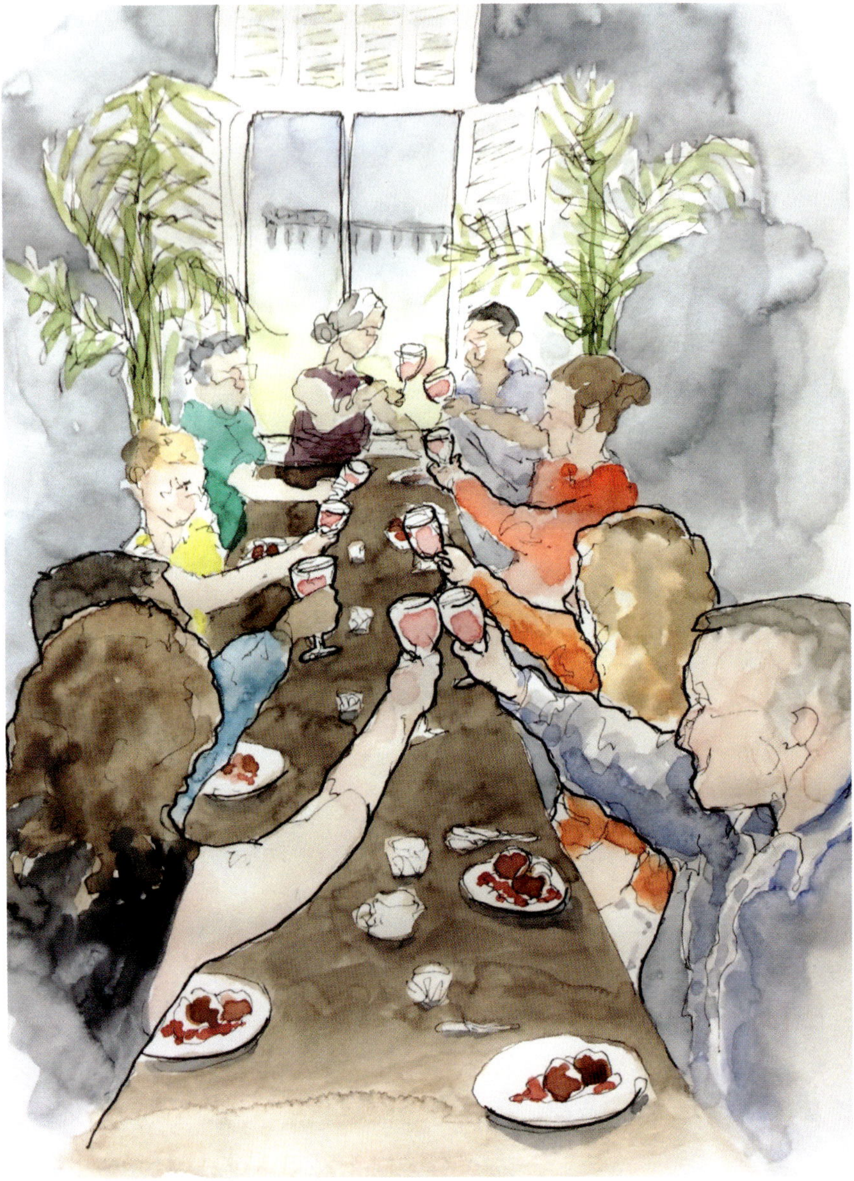

Food Glorious Food

Food is the ingredient that binds us together.

In our busy lives, it seems rarer to gather together for meals and in recent times, we have missed dining with much-loved friends and relatives.

In fact, eating together has many nutritional, health, social and mental benefits. With phones muted and tucked out of sight, we can connect and share in a relaxed way.

The luxury of dining out also includes the added bonus of not having to prepare and wash up – allowing that extra time to savour your meal and company.
The menus at 81 Beach Street reflect the wonderful range, diversity and quality of food served on a daily basis. Put together by one of the most experienced and talented kitchen teams in the area, there is always a great choice of fresh, creative plates; meals that look as good as they taste!

This lovely restaurant also has a private dining room overlooking the English Channel for larger parties or conferences.

You can stroll along the seafront either before or after your visit to really complete the experience.

81 Beach Street, Deal, Kent
www.81beachstreet.co.uk

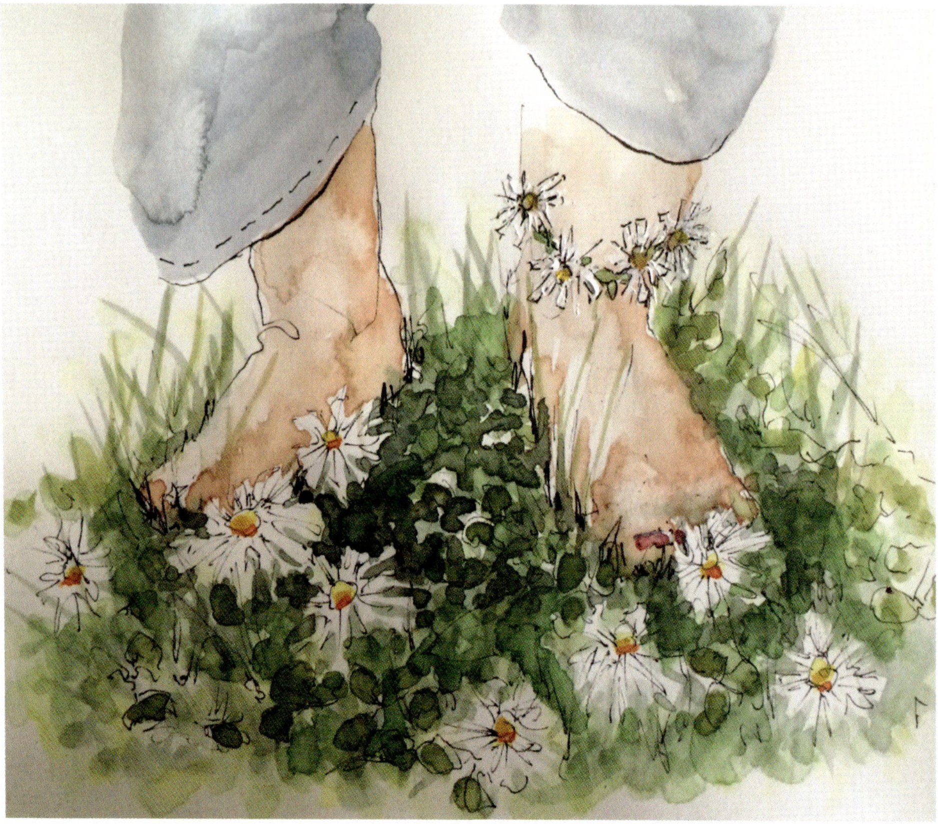

Keep Your Feet on the Ground

Kicking off your shoes (and socks) to go barefoot outside is an instant way to connect with nature.

Walking shoe-free can restore your natural gait and allows your feet the freedom to improve balance and body awareness.

You might not fancy getting your toes cold outdoors in winter but you can certainly still walk around your home with naked feet all year round.

Keeping shoes by the front door can also help keep your home clean and herald your return 'home' after a busy day at work.

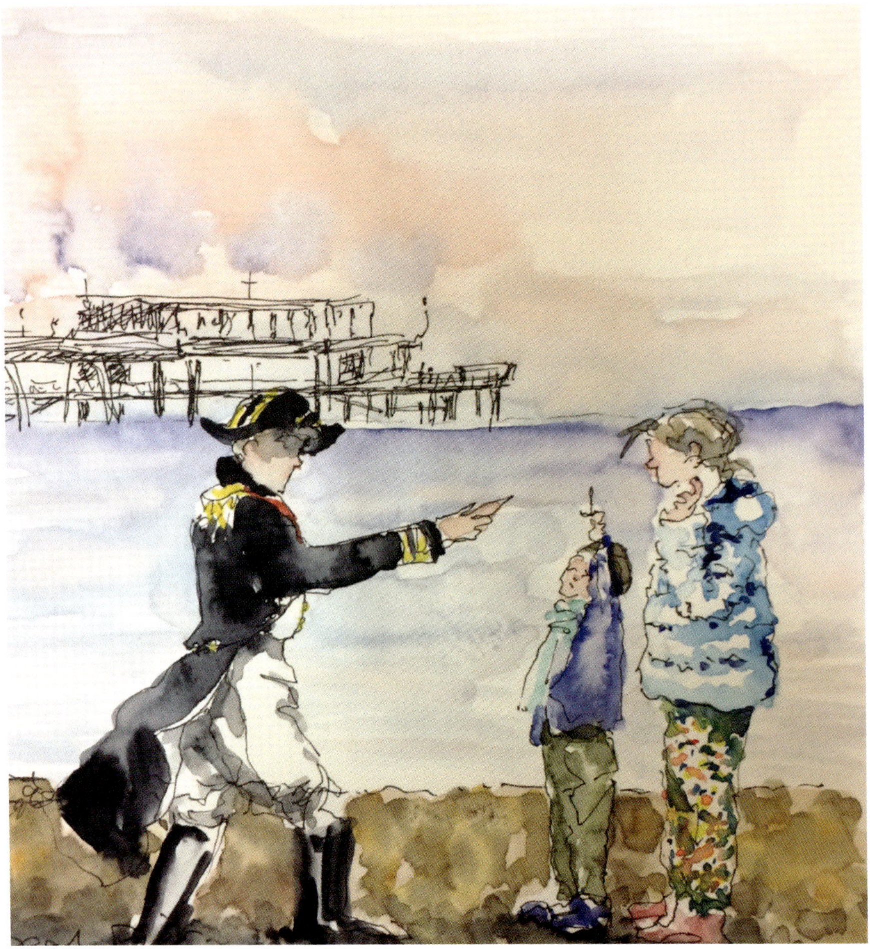

Learn From The Past

Although it is not advisable to dwell on the past for too long, reflecting on past events can uncover valuable life lessons and spark positive ideas for the future.

Looking back in history gives us a sense of context and appreciation for our ancestors who paved the way before us. It can also increase our empathy and understanding of the plight of fellow humans.

The History Project aims to inspire, educate and entertain. Founded by childhood friends George Chittenden and Pete Fishlock who serve the local community by offering Talks, School Workshops and Tours.

Join The History Project on an historic walking tour and delve into Deal's fascinating past.

www.thehistoryproject.co.uk

Follow on Instagram and Facebook!

Best Intentions

Writing things down is undoubtedly a helpful tool in finding clarity about your plans and desired outcomes.

Research has shown that people achieve more if they write down their intentions.

It is also a good idea to be clear about your intentions if they could have an impact on others. For example, if you need to make a difficult decision at home or work, make your intentions known as this gains respect and helps mop up misunderstanding .

Think Nothing Of It

Our minds are constantly chattering.

Find moments in your day to dissolve this incessant commentary by sitting in quiet meditation.

Clearing your mind of thought is definitely something to regularly practice and has extremely therapeutic benefits. Be kind to yourself if your mind wanders- it will do!

Quietly sit, or lay with your eyes closed and seek to just 'be'. We are human be-ings not human do-ings.

Meditation is widely used as a way of reducing negative emotions, increasing creativity and becoming more self-aware. It can help you sleep better and manage stress. Many people link meditation to their ability to problem-solve in both work and home situations.

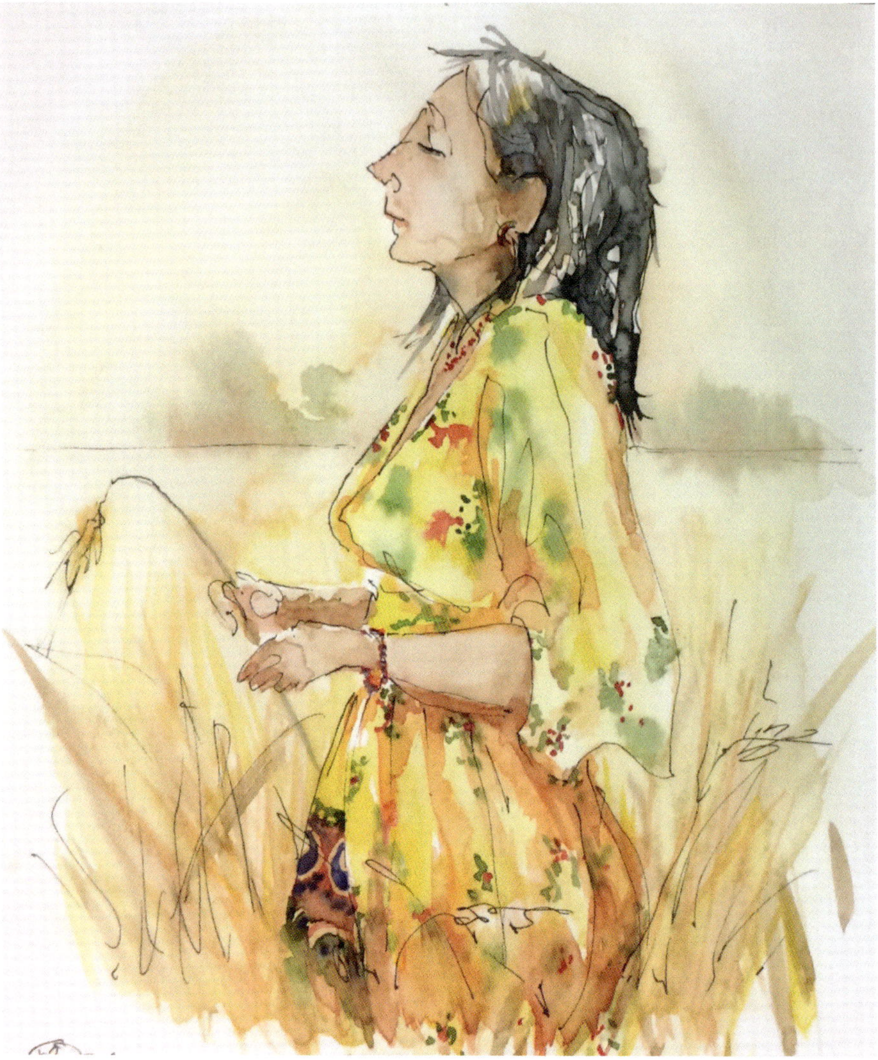

All Dressed Up

Wear what you love and ditch the rest!

Life is too short to save clothes 'for best' and expressing yourself by fashion is empowering and joyous.

Recycling vintage saris and kantha fabrics from across India, Lisa Taylor Design creates luxury clothing, accessories and homewares with a conscious sustainable ethos.

After 25 years at high street brands, designer Lisa Taylor has evolved her own ideas on recycling and hand making to create season-less collections that are eclectic, timeless and beautifully crafted.

Driven by a passion for colour, print and global travel, Lisa continually returns to the vibrancy of her spiritual home, India, for inspiration. Working with local ateliers in Delhi and Jaipur, her vision is brought to life with integrity and energy – inviting you to connect, explore and embark on your own adventure.

www.lisa-taylor.co.uk
Follow on Instagram and Facebook!

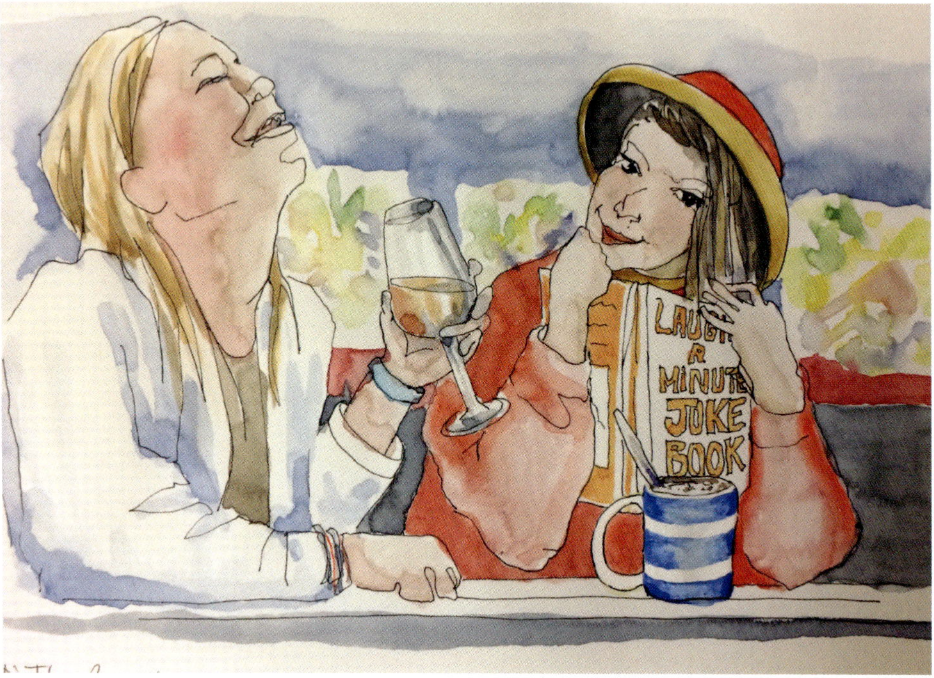
LAUGH A MINUTE JOKE BOOK

Let Friendship Blossom

Take time to nurture real friendships and gently detach from or 'prune' friends you have outgrown.

There is something deeply therapeutic about confiding in a close friend, one who understands you fully and is also not afraid to speak truthfully to you.

A simply gorgeous place to enjoy a glass of something with a friend is The Rose – a hotel, bar and restaurant in Deal, Kent.

Either surrounded by beautiful plants and warm sunshine in the al fresco space in summer, or cosy inside surrounded by stylish furniture and art in the winter, this really is an uber-cool setting to find yourself in.

The Rose has certainly bloomed with great acclaim including being voted as one of the 50 Best Hotels in the UK (Evening Standard, 2020) and in the top 30 Most Romantic UK Hotels (The Times, 2019). It has also been described as one of the top 30 fabulous foodie sleepovers in the UK (The Telegraph, 2020).

91 High Street, Deal

www.therosedeal.com

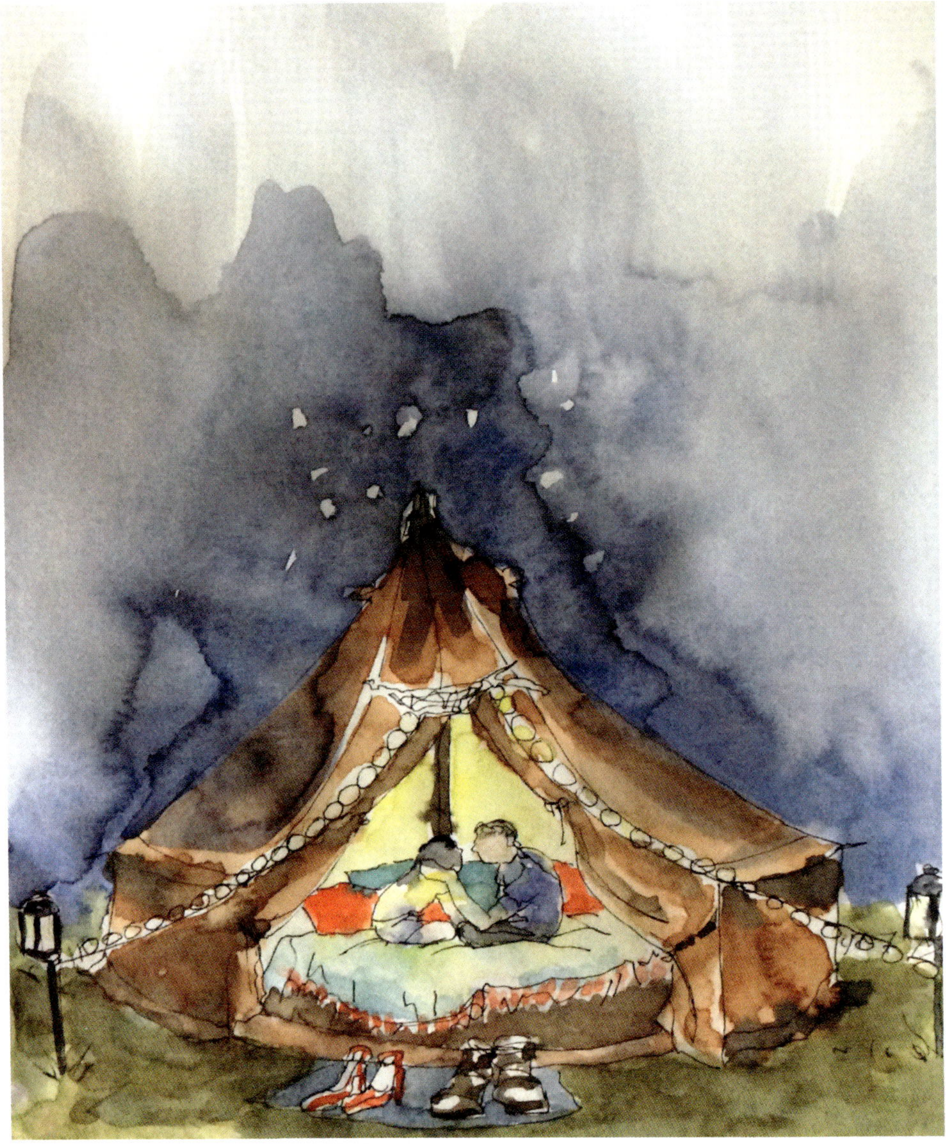

A Blanket of Stars

"I have loved the stars too fondly to be fearful of the night."
Galileo

There is something deeply romantic and magical about spending a night sleeping outside. Listening to the soundtrack of wildlife and resetting your body clock immersed in fresh air is bound to ease the stresses of modern life, making you feel invigorated and alive!

You could spend a night camping in the woods or even in your back garden! This is a low-cost way of really getting back to our roots and letting go. These times can be treasured both alone or with others. Tune in to, and follow, your inner compass to discern what your soul needs right now.

Stars that go supernova are responsible for creating many of the elements of the periodic table, including those that make up the human body. So, science has confirmed that our physical bodies are literally made up from elements originally formed in stars.

We are all stars! Shine bright!

Honour Your Ancestors

"Each time my feet touched the earth I knew my mother was there with me. I knew this body was not mine alone, but a living continuation of my mother and all of my ancestors. These feet that I saw as 'my' feet were actually 'our' feet. Together, my mother and I were leaving footprints in the damp soil."
Thich Nhat Hanh

How much do you know about your family tree?

It may not be possible for you, but if you can, trace back your family history. You may uncover fascinating details about your ancestors. Perhaps, you discover that there have been recurring themes in terms of health or career choices! These people made sacrifices and have gifted us in so many ways.

Display photographs of family members who have passed over and be a reliable guardian of any family heirlooms. You may choose to remember significant dates – such as birth dates, passings or wedding anniversaries - and mark them in your own special way.

In this way, we honour and pay our respects to those who walked this Earth before us.

Learn to say NO

"This above all: to thine own self be true,
And it must follow, as the night the day,
Thou canst not then be false to any man."
Shakespeare

Establishing healthy boundaries is an important aspect of all relationships and sometimes we have to just say 'no'. Finding a comfortable space to be honest enables others to have clarity in their expectations and provides you with control and empowerment.

Your life is not supposed to be lived solely fulfilling the wishes of others if it causes resentment and frustration.

If you start saying 'no', you may find you gain greater respect from people who wiill appreciate your candour and confidence.

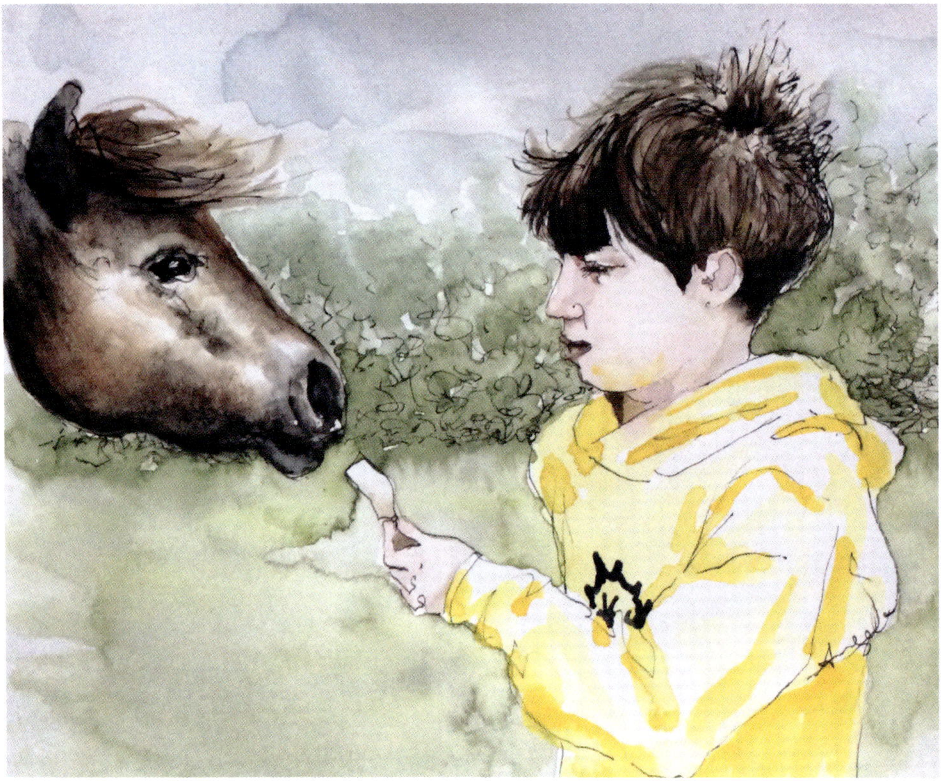

Animal Instincts

"Some people talk to animals. Not many listen though. That's the problem."
A.A. Milne

The upside of having a pet is fairly well-documented with claims that pets can help us live longer, reduce stress, lower blood pressure, provide comfort and companionship.

Some pets encourage us to get outside more and this could lead to improved fitness and opportunities to socialise. The more spiritually-minded among us recognize that animals can sense when something is wrong and offer protection and guidance in times of crisis.

It may just be that your pet helps you to stay playful and present.

For many of us, having our own pet is not an option but there are still plenty of ways we can reap the rewards of interacting with all creatures great and small. We could take a neighbour's dog for a walk, encourage birds to visit our garden by enticing them with nourishment, we can support animal charities and honour the animal kingdom by treating animals with care and respect.

In any case, love animals and hold on to your right to horse around!

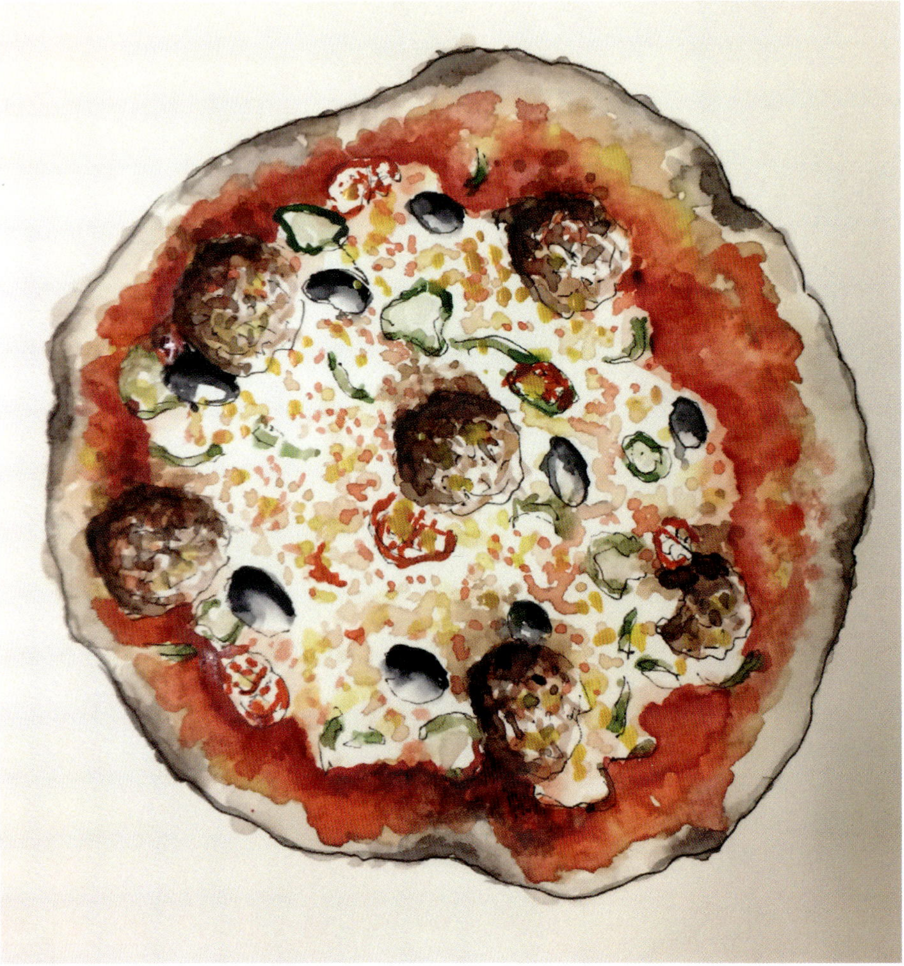

Feed Your Soul

"One cannot think well, love well, sleep well, if one has not dined well."
Virginia Woolf

According to Wikipedia, the word 'pizza' was first documented in 997 A.D. Modern pizza was eaten in Central and Southern Italy in the 16th century, when poor Neapolitans would eat this 'street food' al fresco and often whilst walking around. This is because they had little space in their one-room homes.

Using only the finest fresh ingredients, The Hayman's Kitchen supply rustic sourdough pizza in a tiny, family-run restaurant. The adventure started in 2015 and this unique business oozes amore!

The Hayman's Kitchen

352 Dover Road, Walmer, Deal

Find them on Facebook!

Meet Your Mentor

A mentor can appear in your life from a variety of avenues. Perhaps they are your old school teacher or university lecturer. They might be a more senior colleague at work or a much-loved friend of the family.

Identify the mentors in your life and make sure you show them appreciation for the advice and support they may have gifted you.

Being a mentor to someone is also a truly fulfilling experience which allows us the sense of 'giving back' or 'paying forward' the generosity of spirit we have gratefully received. There could be a student who would love your career advice or a more junior employee in need of guidance and tips. A word of gentle warning, these relationships will emerge organically so there is no need to pursue!

Digital Detox

How many of us spend far too much time entwined with our digital devices?

We may need technology for work and general life but sometimes we should switch the controls!

Try putting your phone on silent and (if you need to) check it at regular intervals on YOUR Terms. This alleviates that sense of constantly feeling like you are 'on call' and places the control firmly back in your hands.

It might be time to think about setting some healthy and realistic boundaries in relation to your time spent on social media and refrain from using phones and laptops in the bedroom!

Having some time out from technology really allows us to recharge and interact with our fellow humans. If you can unplug for a bit of time each day then you might gain that valuable time for getting out in nature, exercising, mindfulness and making memories with loved ones.

Disconnect to reconnect...

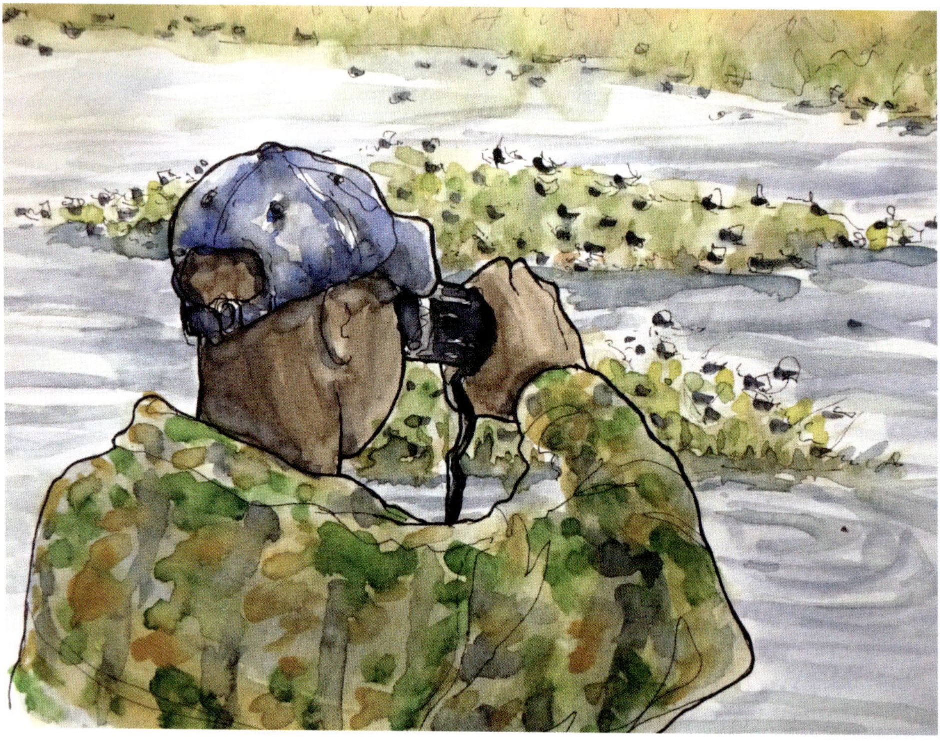

Oberve & Listen

When watching a robin checking you out on a nearby branch, or a flock of 200 Lapwing taking flight, their alien calls and swooping movements above you, your mind clears and nothing else matters.

Whether in the middle of the countryside or a town, birds are all around us, and taking a minute to watch and listen to these wild animals adds a sense of calm and intrigue to your day.

Birdsong itself can transcend you to other places and can help reduce stress. You could even learn some of the songs and enhance your wanders by knowing a little bit more about the world around you.

Spending time watching and listening to these wonderfully diverse animals opens up a whole new aspect of life.

Each glance out a window is improved, each trip to the shop is made better by identifying each species you see.

info@sbbot.org.uk
Sandwich Bay Bird Observatory Trust
Guilford Rd, Sandwich Bay, Kent, CT13 9PF

See what is happening by visiting our website: www.sbbot.org.uk

You can also follow on Facebook or Twitter.

Sing a Song

"A bird does not sing because it has an answer. It sings because it has a song."
Chinese Proverb

Humans have been singing since time began and there is no culture, however isolated or remote that doesn't sing.

You might reserve your singing to the shower or revel in belting out some tunes in a drunken karaoke session. Perhaps it's more your thing to sing in a church choir or softly sing lullabies to your new-born baby.

Singing can have a host of health benefits for body and mind. Through using the breath it can improve posture, lower stress levels and be a workout for your lungs, throat and mouth!

Belting out a tune can increase mental alertness, broaden communication skills, aid decent sleep and widen your circle of friends.

Whether it's just confined to the shower, singing is really good for the soul.

No Right or Wrong

"There is nothing either good or bad, but thinking makes it so."
Shakespeare

We have given things labels of "this is right" and "this is wrong" ... it is really helpful to come to the understanding that this is neither fixed or universal.

As humans, we cannot always see the Bigger Picture but we can endeavour to understand that everything is subject to the labels we have given them based on a wider context.

If you catch yourself passing judgement, take some time to notice why and whether your reaction is impacting negatively on others and yourself.

Look for the good in people.

Make Do & Mend

Make Do and Mend was a pamphlet issued by the British Ministry of Information in the midst of World War II.

The intention was to offer thrifty design ideas and advice on revamping worn clothing. These frugal-thinking ideas included creating attractive, decorative patches to cover holes, unpicking old jumpers in order to re-knit chic alternatives and tips on altering men's clothes to be suitable to be worn by women.

This approach to clothing (and all other household items) is a great way to reduce your carbon footprint, save money and ensure you stand out from the crowd!

Next time you are about to ditch something, consider if it can be given a new lease of life!

Nod Off

"Sleep is the best meditation."
Dalai Lama

There is no doubt about it, having a good night's sleep is an excellent way to avoid getting out of the wrong side of the bed!

Widely-accepted tips on getting a good 40 winks include simply taking the time to relax, establishing a routine and avoiding certain food and drinks before bedtime (such as spicy or sugary food, alcohol or coffee.) Maintaining a healthy lifestyle – by exercising and eating well - also contribute.
Aim to create a calm, dark and uncluttered environment free from technology.

Waking up each morning feeling well-rested is a great way of looking after both your physical and mental health.

Sweet Dreams.

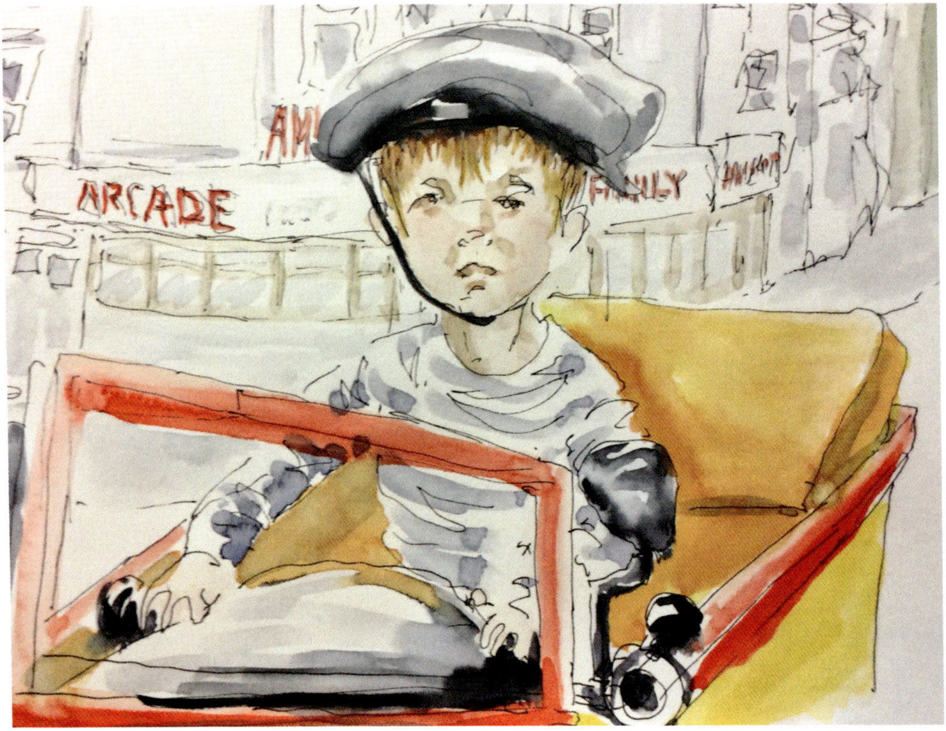
ARCADE

Young At Heart

"Growing old is mandatory, but growing up is optional."
Walt Disney

You have a choice: You can choose to be forever young!

A few signs that you are already well on your way are the ability to see humour in life. Try not to take yourself or others too seriously.

Do you try new things and ignore fear? Children are often jaw-droppingly fearless!

Get outside and immerse yourself in the wonders of the natural world!

Make new friends and live for today... age ain't nothing but a number!

The Art of Re-Framing

Every situation can be viewed from a variety of angles.

When you are feeling negative emotions about an issue, try to reframe it in your favour.

If your friend is late to meet you in town, enjoy window shopping for a few minutes.

A broken favourite coffee cup is a perfect excuse to treat yourself to a new one.

If you lose your job, see it as an opportunity to work on your home and re-align with your purpose.

If you are unable to control the problem then try to look at it through different lenses.

Laugh It Off

"A day without laughter is a day wasted."
Charlie Chaplin

It is often said that laughter is the best medicine and there is evidence to support the fact that it strengthens our immune system and protects against the damaging effects of stress.

Having a laugh with friends can galvanise your relationship and lift your spirits – even in dark and difficult times.

Prescribe yourself with curling up on the sofa to watch your favourite comedy or a catch up with a pal who never fails to make you giggle.

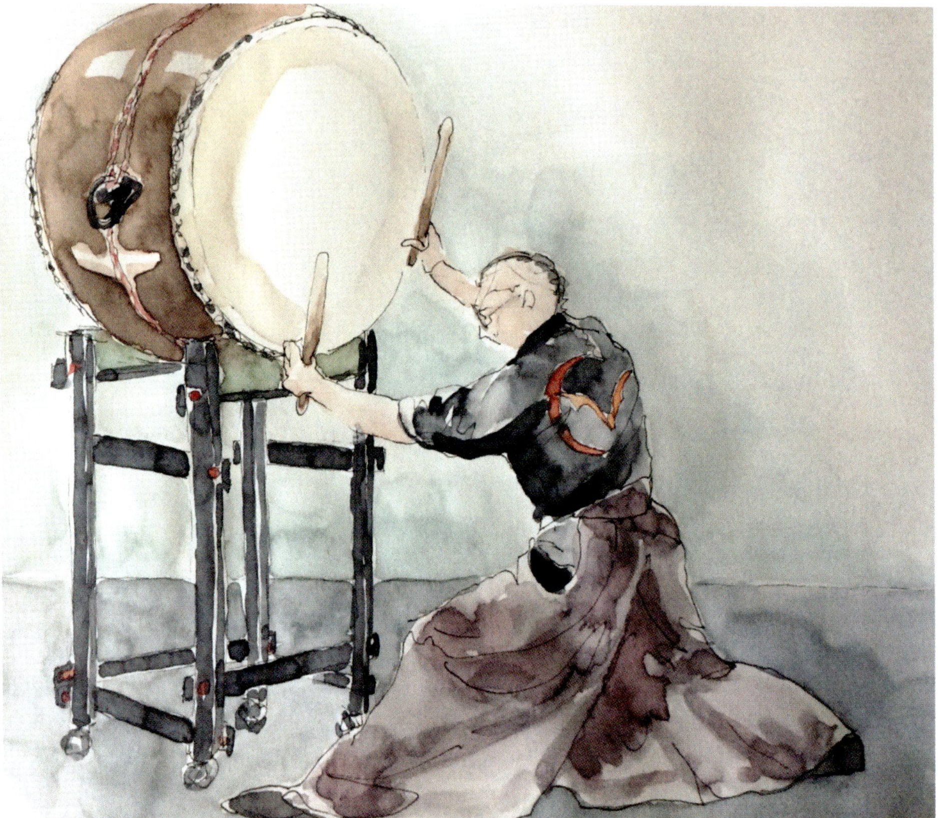

Beat Your Own Drum

Kensei Taiko

Taiko...Japanese drumming is communal drumming on huge traditional drums with big body movements and specific stances! Practiced since the dawn of Japanese civilization, the deep beat of the taiko pervades the depths of the bamboo forests and our being...

The rhythms are based in nature, and the whole experience has enormous benefits for physical, mental and spiritual wellbeing. Feeling energised, elated and stimulated are the results of a taiko workshop!

Anyone can partake, working within their own limits and can even join performance bands to play at events.

William's path to teaching taiko originated in the Japanese sword martial art, iaijutsu and thence into taiko which he has been teaching for around 20 years.

Taiko requires respect, cooperation, tolerance and fellowship; it builds communities, self-esteem, teamwork and a sense of humour...try it, you'll love it!

Contact William, Shihan:
kenseitaiko@gmail.com
Find them on Facebook!

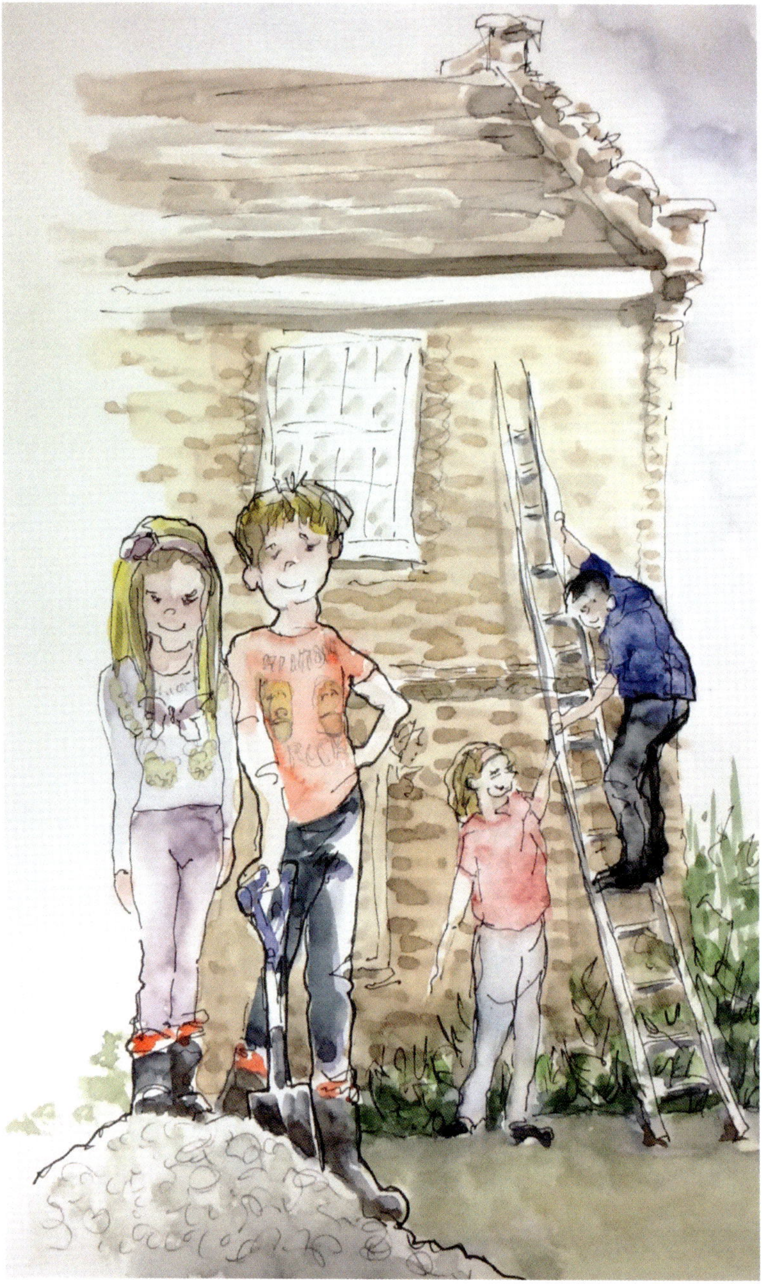

Get Your House in Order

Letter to your house:

Let's have a deal:
Your owners fell for your charms, promise and feel.
Let's be honest, we all need to be friends: the homeowner, the builder and your problems (they're real).
Your owners are hoping to be with you - stay until their lives end.
Please be safe, welcoming and full of joy,
(Especially for your owners' little girl and boy).
Working on you, we promise to shower you with the utmost attention,
Even if you have a bit more woodworm than we care to mention.
We promise to work tirelessly to make sure you are fit,
and correct you - sympathetically - little bit by bit.
Please do not fight me. I have your survival in mind, I'm asking you to provide shelter for your family: all snuggly and kind.
When working on you, please bring everything to hand,
I promise you, House, to make you happy along with all of your Land.
We get very excited working on you, House.
I love everything about it - even the odd mouse!

Dickinson & Son
Building and property maintenance for work on your house.
For further info, find them on Facebook!

Just Passing Through

It can be very liberating and calming to remember our time on Planet Earth (in our current physical form) is temporary and transitory.

Live each day as if it might be your last but avoid feeling fearful of death.

Contemplate how you would like to be remembered by friends and family when your spirit has been set free from the body.

What will be the legacy you leave behind of your time here?

Walk on the Wild Side

And if the world has ceased to hear you,
Say to the silent earth:
I flow.
To the rushing water, speak:
I am.
Rilke

Go on a nature walk in some woodland, coastline or near a river or waterfall.

Observe and interact with the elements. Listen to the sound of the wind in the trees, the branches underfoot, birds twittering away or the waves crashing on the shore.

When we use the word 'wild' we often think of the definition of lacking restraint in behaviour - perhaps at parties and festivals. Whilst this is one meaning, we should remember our natural wild nature.

To feel native, untamed, undomesticated, feral, indigenous and savage in a natural habitat brimming with the planet's diverse and abundant resources and creatures is a guaranteed way of nourishing your soul.

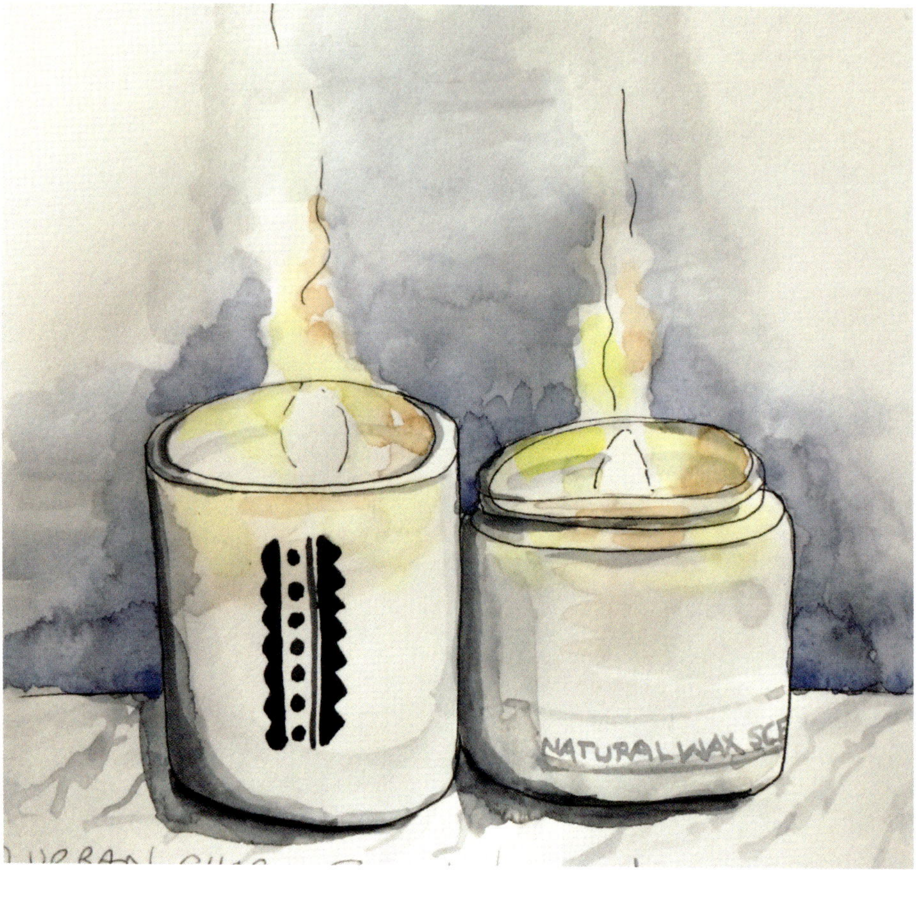
NATURAL WAX SCE

Shed Light on a Matter

Lighting a candle is a simple part of your self-care routine, enabling you to connect with the elements to bring a sense of comfort and calm.

Candles have been used for centuries in sacred ceremonies and rituals. You can borrow this idea regardless of your own religious or spiritual beliefs as a mindfulness practice by lighting a candle and observing the flicker of the flame and the smell (if it is scented).

You may want to set an intention or say a prayer when lighting a candle and make sure your phone is out of sight.

If you want to spark some passion, candles are a hands down winner. When you are attracted to someone, your pupils dilate. Well…candlelight causes pupils to dilate! So this, coupled with the intimacy candlelight creates, sets the scene for a romantic night.

Urban Chic is a vintage-inspired boutique which stocks a range of thoughtfully selected women's clothing, accessories, beauty and gifts including candles.

The Urban Chic sisters, Claire and Dawn, curate a bespoke collection of high quality basics alongside more unique pieces.

Urban Chic

67 High Street, Deal

Follow on Instagram and Facebook!

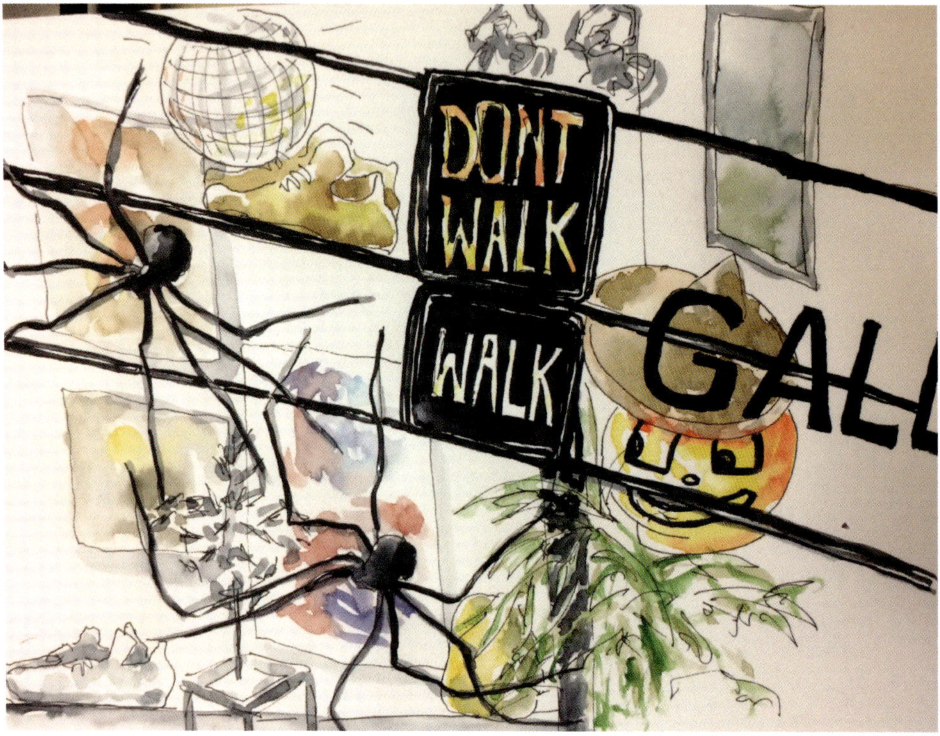
DON'T
WALK
WALK

Eye Candy

"Art washes away from the soul the dust of everyday life."
Picasso

Picture this:

Something urges you to take a walk down to the 'wrong' end of town and you end up in an art gallery, down a side road off the beaten track. You could be anywhere, but wherever that is, you feel you are where it's AT.

It is no secret that art has the power to provoke thought or provide relief and a sense of escapism. Viewing art can be a way of improving your mood and potentially increasing empathy for others. Visiting an art gallery is a fantastic way of feeling a part of the creative community and adding a flash of invigoration and inspiration to your day!

DON'T WALK WALK is an independent artist run gallery in Deal, Kent. The gallery, owned by Neil (Ned) Kelly, boasts a 'punk rock' ethic and showcases a wide range of works from both emerging and established artists.

Deal is one lucky town with this on the doorstep...

DON'T WALK WALK GALLERY

10 Victoria Road, Deal

www.dontwalkwalkgallery.com

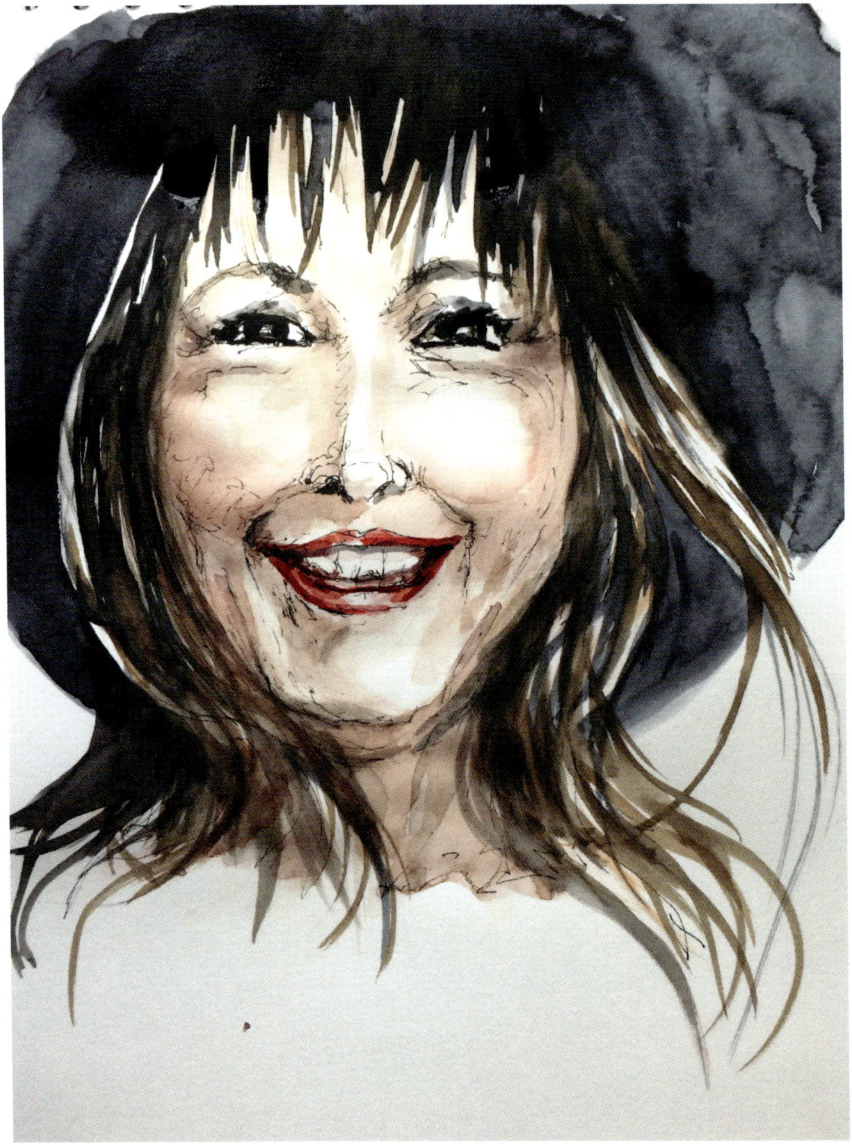

Smiley Face

"Life is like a mirror. Smile at it and it smiles back at you."
Peace Pilgrim

It might be a cheeky smirk, wide grin or gentle beam… smiling is a beautiful way to brighten up the world!

Smiling has many positive health and wellbeing benefits and simply choosing to smile can actually trick your brain into feeling happier! You can also make new friends, improve your career prospects or find love!

Did you know World Smile Day is celebrated on the first Friday in October?

Set yourself a challenge today to smile at or greet at least one stranger!

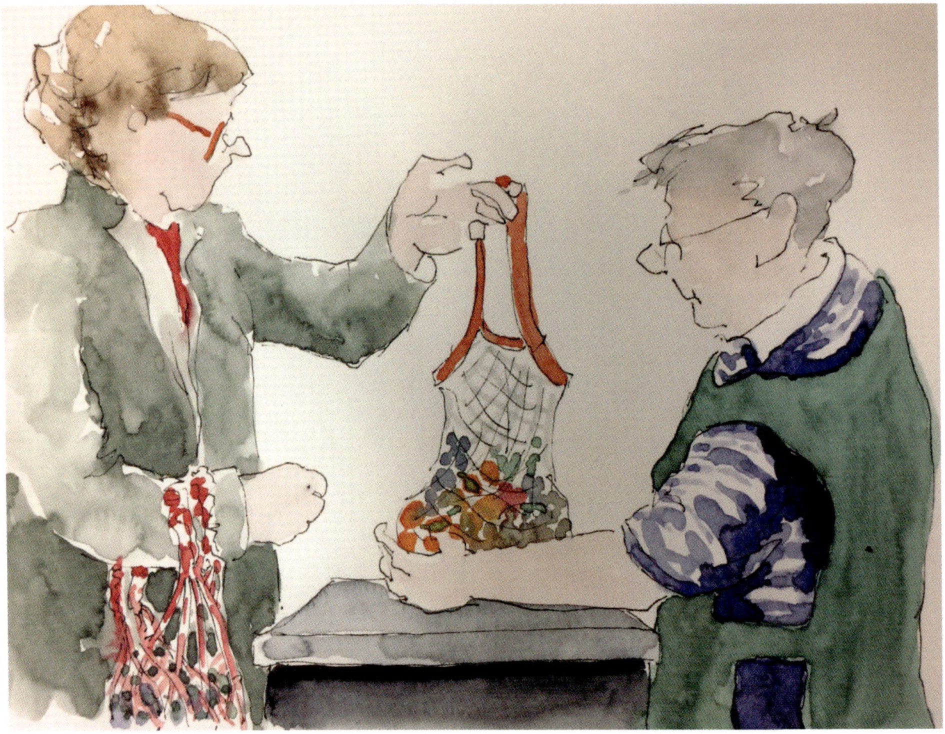

Sharing is Caring

"Even the smallest kindness shall not be forgotten."
Japanese Proverb

Acts of kindness where possible enrich our lives and strengthen our sense of community.

"We don't think anyone in our community should have to face going hungry. That's why we provide three days' nutritionally balanced emergency food and support to local people who are referred to us in crisis. We are part of a nationwide network of foodbanks, supported by The Trussell Trust, working to combat poverty and hunger across the UK."

Deal Area Foodbank

www.dealarea.foodbank.org.uk

Avoid Gossip

"Who gossips to you, will gossip of you."
Turkish Proverb

Gossip can be defined as 'idle talk' or rumour about the private or personal affairs of others.

There are times when it is necessary to mention or discuss others when they are not present (perhaps in a work context or chat with a family member or close friend) but it is unkind to talk badly of others.

Oftentimes, if you are gossiping about others, it could be a red flag that you are distracting yourself from issues within your own life. Have a check in and see if the behaviour of others is triggering you in some way and why. Don't beat yourself up – we have all partaken in gossip. Just become aware and change the subject or remove yourself from conversations which gravitate towards complaining about others.

Truly contented souls do not waste their valuable time and energy on gossip.

Break the Habit

As humans, we can all be creatures of habit which can provide a sense of routine and comfort.

However, if you always walk the same way to work, shop in the same supermarket or order the same dish in your favourite restaurant then challenge yourself to mix it up!

Variety is the spice of life and you will be pleasantly surprised to see the world through new lenses (even if you do stay in the same town)!

What can you do today that is a break from the norm?

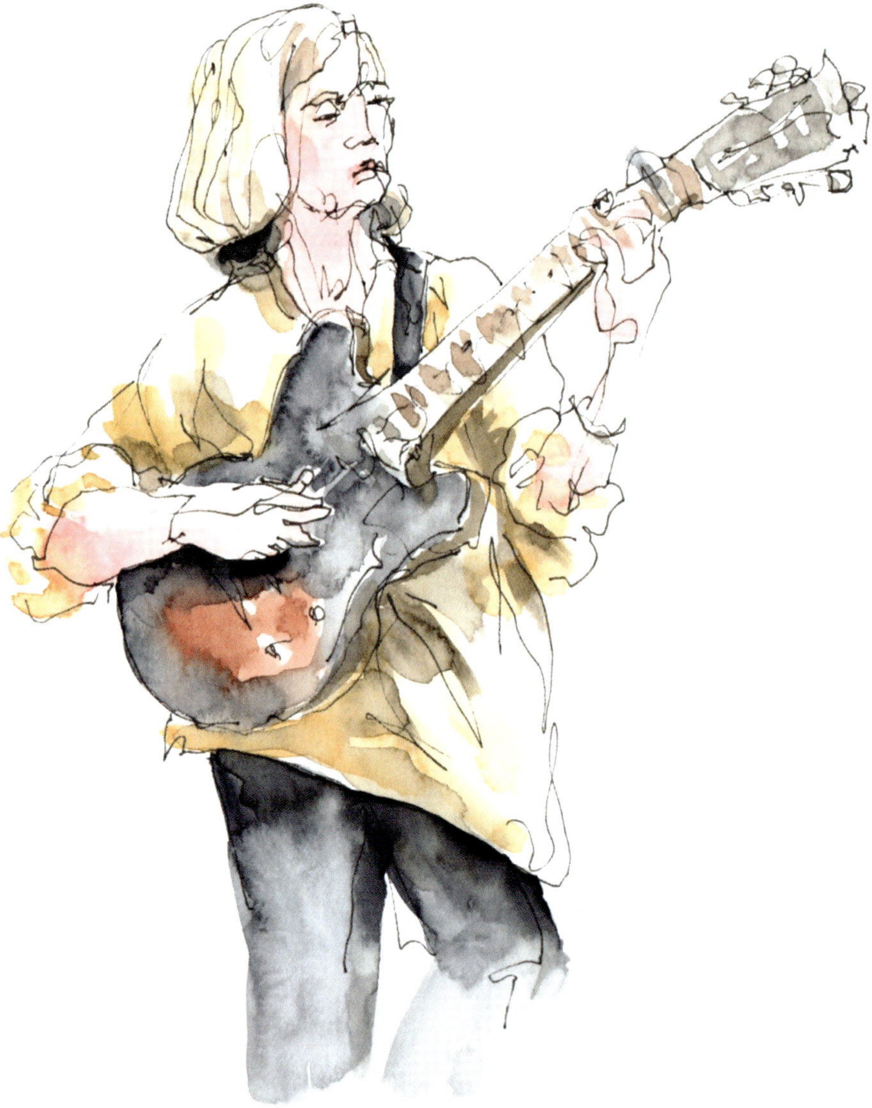

Play On

"If music be the food of love, play on"
Shakespeare

Gathering to listen to live music is a collective mood-boosting experience which nourishes the individual soul and wider community.

Research has concluded that live music can reduce stress, making us feel happier and more engaged.

Run by a family team of musicians, artists, designers, sound engineers and expert bar people in Deal, The Lighthouse has a fully-equipped stage and sound-system, with a passionate in-house sound team.

The Lighthouse strives to bring an eclectic mix of music and creative events, hosting amazing artists from around the country and beyond.

To The Lighthouse!

The Lighthouse Music & Arts Pub
50 The Strand, Walmer, Deal

www.thelighthousedeal.co.uk

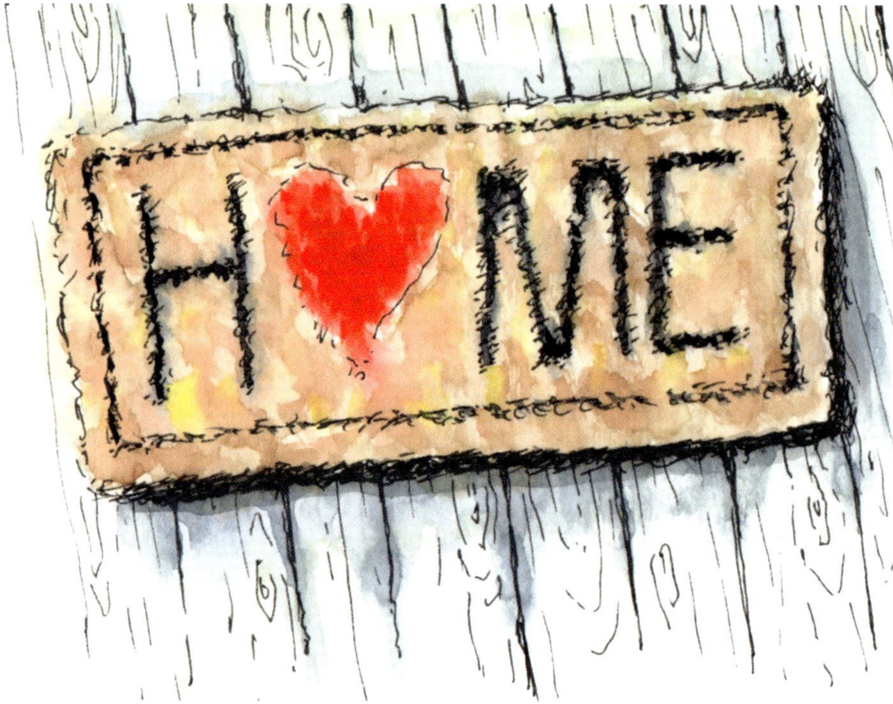

H♥ME

Home Sweet Home

If you are not yet on the Property Ladder: don't fret. There are several advantages to being a tenant - such as greater geographical freedom and having someone to call if the boiler has broken or the roof is leaking! Perhaps, you are a homeowner in a position to become a landlord.

Either way, established in 1990, Deal Rental Bureau is the only dedicated and fully independent residential lettings specialist for Deal and the surrounding areas.

Get in touch with their friendly team to discuss your needs!

Deal Rental Bureau

1 Stanhope Road, Deal

www.dealrentalbureau.co.uk

Waste Not, Want Not

Limiting the amount of waste we produce is bound to have a positive effect on our planet.

By using less water, turning off lights, being economic with food and curbing unnecessary consumerism we can all 'do our bit' for the world.

Adopting a frugal way of life can actually be fun and creative whilst saving money too!

Big Girls (& Boys) Do Cry

It's OK to cry. Don't be ashamed.

Us humans are the only animals to cry tears of sadness and scientists have discovered that shedding a few tears can make you feel better in the long run.

Crying is a way of releasing strong emotional feelings such as grief, anger and joy. There are three types of tears: reflex tears, continuous tears and emotional tears. Whilst reflex and continuous tears are more about clearing debris and lubricating the eyes, emotional tears contain stress hormones and toxins which seek release from the body.

After a few minutes of crying, you often feel the body's self-soothing mechanisms kick in and you might start to feel a bit numb. This is how weeping can help you find a place of calm.

Crying can help you process big life changes such as the loss of a loved one or the breakdown of a marriage.

Allowing others to see you in a more vulnerable emotional state can bring awareness to a situation and motivate friends and family to support and help.

Having said all of this, should you find yourself crying regularly and it is coupled with sense of hopelessness or thoughts of suicide then please reach out for professional help.

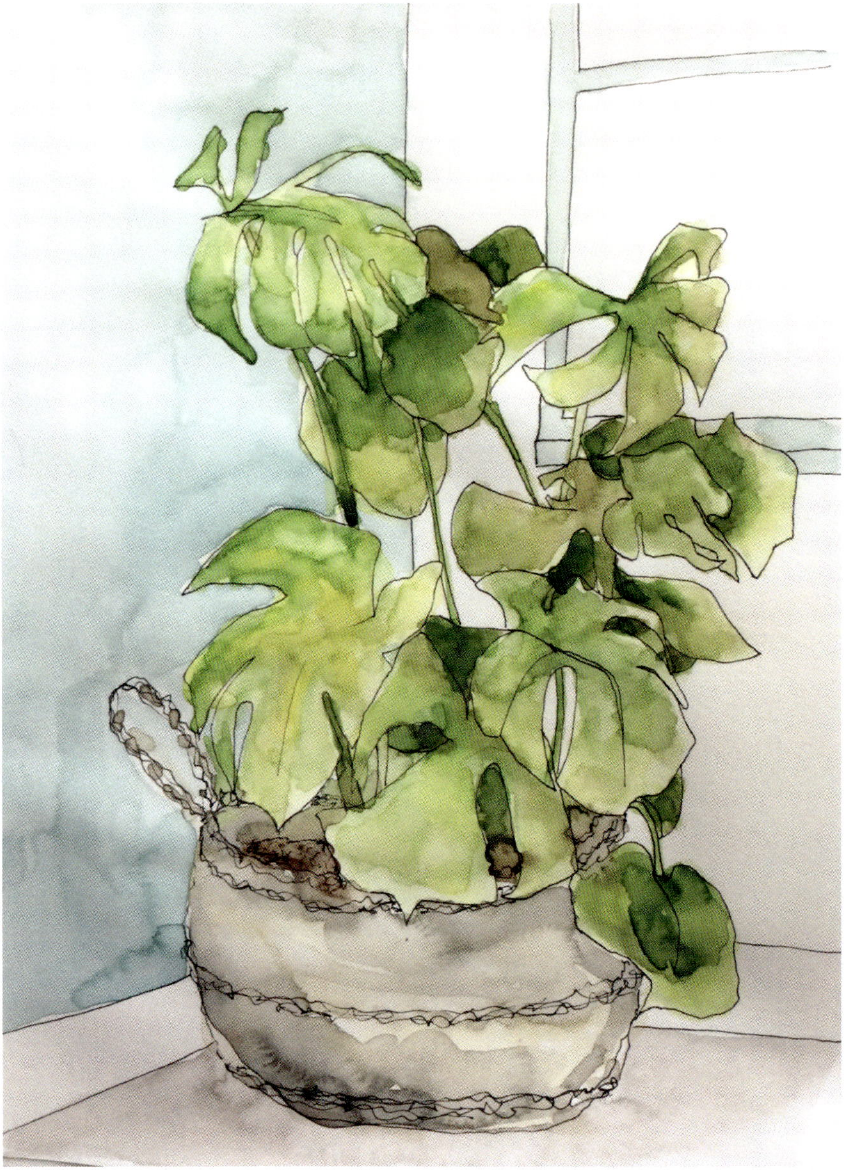

Plant Power

There are huge health and wellbeing benefits to bringing a bit of the outside in!

Surrounding yourself with houseplants has been linked to improving your mood and reducing stress.

Adding some plants to your home not only brings beauty to your living environment but also helps to improve air quality. Some might also say that the plants in their home boost productivity, creativity and sharpen their focus.

In recent times, it has been necessary for us to spend lengthy times indoors so there has been an opportunity – or instinct - to create a sanctuary for peace and healing at home.

Sharing your home with plants just feels a bit happier and healthier – especially if you talk to them!

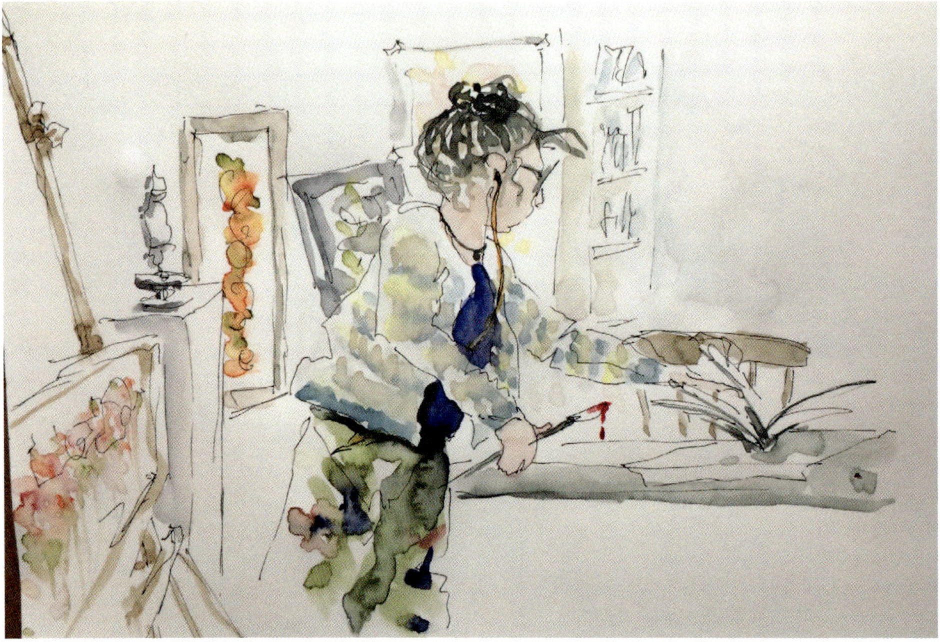

Creative Spirit

As adults, we might frequently encourage our children and young people to be creative in Art, Music or Drama. We may have fond childhood memories of painting messy artworks, dancing or perhaps performing in the school play.

Creativity is not just reserved for children and creative professionals: it is for everyone.

We are creative every day by choosing the words we speak, the clothes we wear and the food we eat.

Getting in touch with your creative spirit is a fantastic way of expressing yourself and reducing stress and anxiety. Creative pursuits can improve your ability to problem-solve, provide a sense of purpose and bring excitement and enthusiasm into your life!

Humans are naturally creative. It is our birthright.

www.ohmalones.com

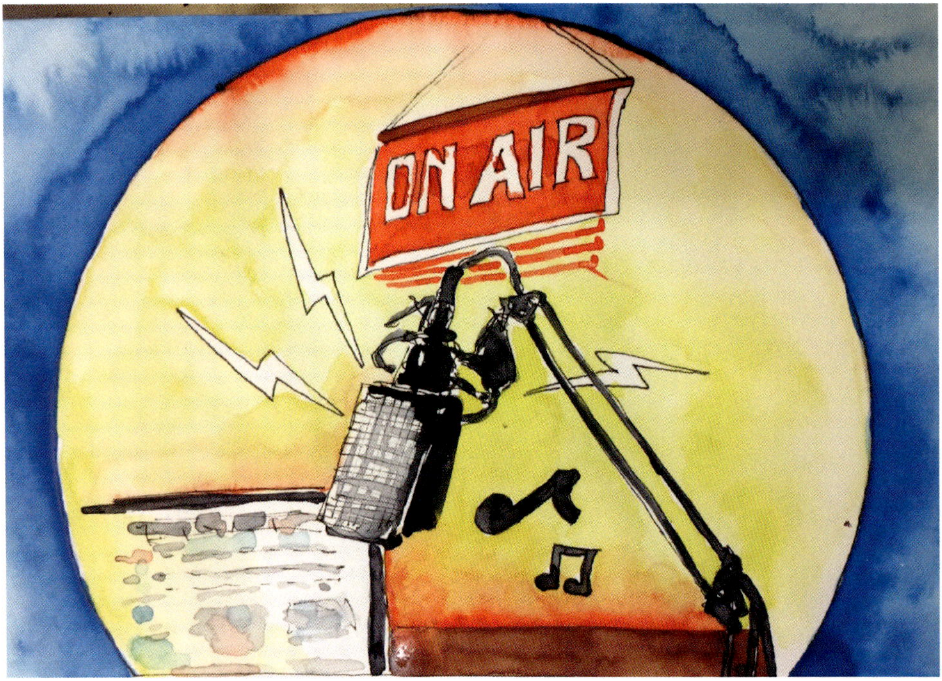
ON AIR

Tune in to your Tribe

There are powerful emotional benefits to tuning into the radio, such as improving your mood and escaping life's pressures.

Radio keeps listener's company too, which is a brilliant way to help combat loneliness. One key advantage of radio is the ability to focus on local issues where necessary.

Deal Radio aims to deliver a focused resource for the development of community education, entertainment and empowerment.

DR wants the whole community to get involved in this great venture.

"Listen in, phone in, contribute, visit us, dance with us, be with us."

Deal Radio
Broadcast Studios

The Landmark Centre, Deal

www.dealradio.co.uk

Have a Staycation

Recent events have led us to consider our holiday options at home.

This can be viewed as an opportunity to be a tourist in your own town!

The many advantages also include: less time travelling (definitely no jet lag!), saves money and zero frustrating squeeze-everything-into-a-suitcase moments! It is also kinder to the planet due to less carbon emissions and you can even 'bring' your pets!

Top tips: tidy away clutter, treat yourself to some special food, start with clean towels and fresh linen, place beautiful flowers in a vase, source some luxury pamper items such as a face mask or bath bombs. If you usually purchase magazines or new books to read whilst away - still do that! Why not use this as a chance to explore local attractions you have never visited?

Whatever you do, avoid the temptation to bung a laundry load in or pick up a work email!

Just think...you could do this every weekend!

Choose to Cheerlead!

Identify those around you whom you whole-heartedly support and then... make a song and dance about it!

This could be your favourite restaurant, author, hairdresser, independent clothes shop or therapist.

Individuals and businesses dine out on fellow humans singing their praises and will be so grateful for your support and kindness. You can do this by liking, sharing or commenting on social media or perhaps writing someone a glowing reference, testimonial or review.

Just. Spread. The. Love.

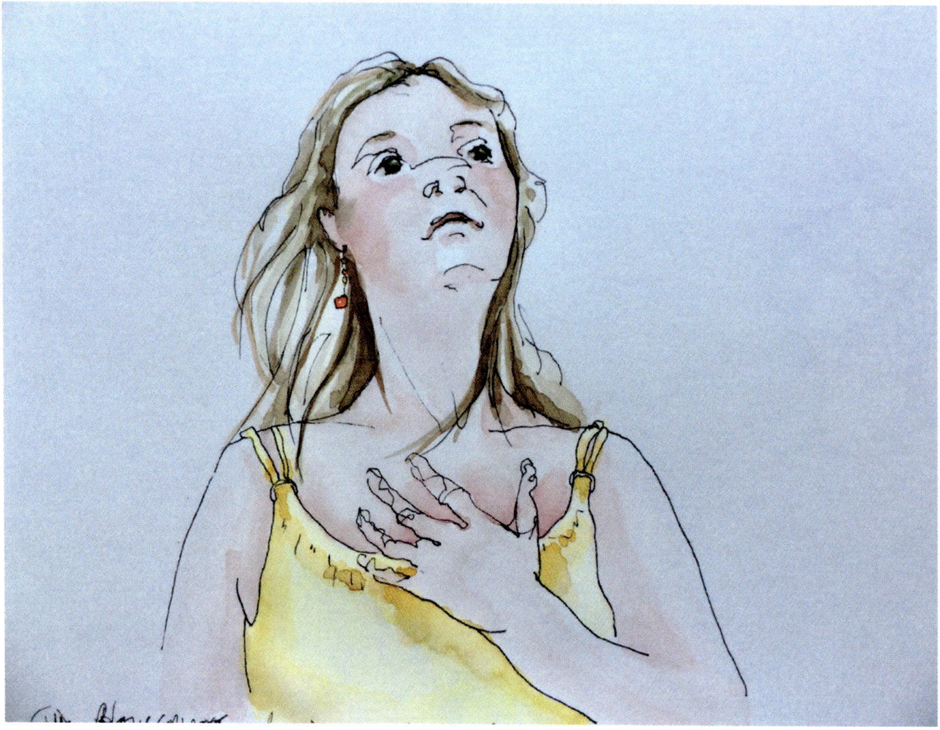

Hand on Heart

The human heart is the universal symbol for love and it is believed by many to be the seat of the soul or spirit and the centre of happiness.

To say the heart is powerful is the understatement of a lifetime. It is just the size of a fist but can pump blood to every cell in your body in under a minute.

Take a moment to place a hand on your heart.

This simple act brings awareness and acknowledgement. Notice how that touch brings instant calm.

Close your eyes and thank your heart.

Promise to trust and honour it ...always.

Lifelong Learners

"Education is not the learning of facts but the training of the mind to think."
Albert Einstein

Approaching life with an inquisitive mind is a sure-fire way to keep mentally active and stimulated.

This book has made reference to a few concepts and ideas you might find intriguing so here is a list of a few books you may want to delve into at some point:

The Miracle of Mindfulness by Thich Nhat Hanh

The Power of Now & A New Earth by Eckhart Tolle

The Surrender Experiment by Michael A Singer

Clear Your Clutter with Feng Shui by Karen Kingston

The Art of Dying by Peter & Elizabeth Fenwick

The Secret (& other titles) by Rhonda Byrne

You Are A Goddess by Sophie Bashford

The True Power of Water by Masaru Emoto

The Hidden Life of Trees by Peter Wohlleben

Trust Your Gut

"Trust your instincts. Intuition doesn't lie."
Oprah Winfrey

We are all born with an internal compass and we should ignore this at our peril.

Sometimes in life, we just have a 'feeling' or 'hunch' about something and you are serving yourself well if you at least listen to, or heed your own guidance system.

Following your inner voice can take courage and fearlessness but it is certainly a way to honour your mind, body and soul.

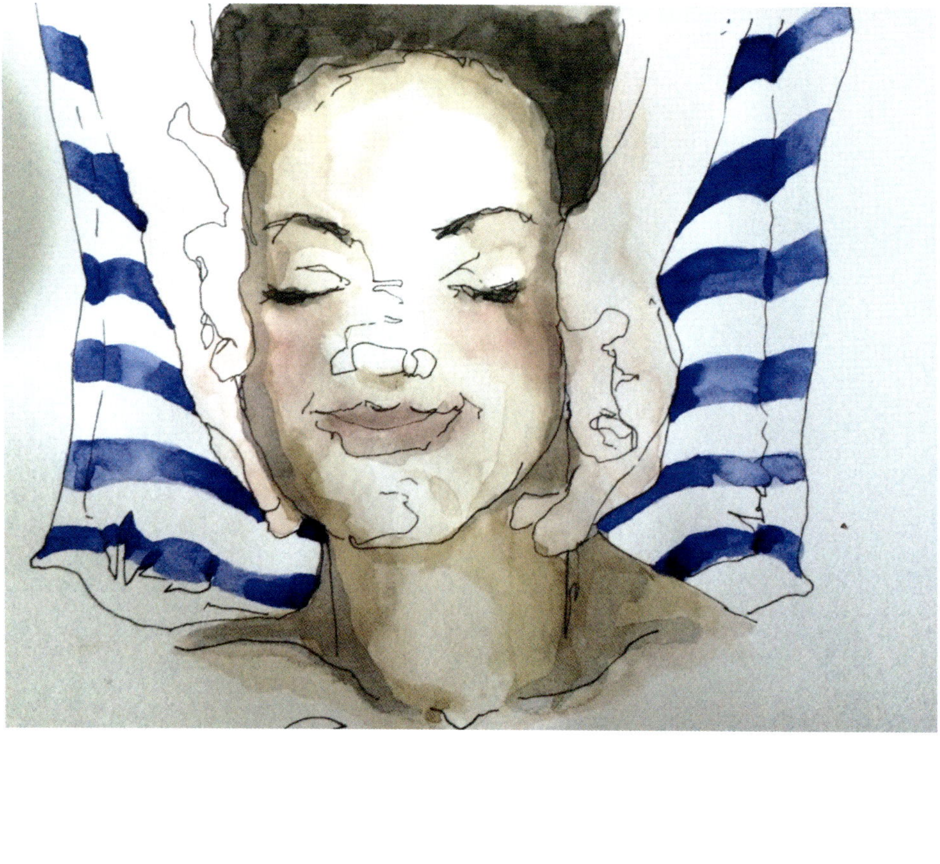

Love the Skin You're In

Not only does massage help improve circulation and release toxins from the body, it is also about sending positive signals to your physical form that it is loved and safe.

After years working for others in the Spa Industry, Sarah saw an opportunity to build a studio in her Deal garden and launch her own business. Daisy Green Skincare Studio was born and it was the best move she ever made.

Daisy Green has a passionate focus on plant-based products and a more natural approach to skincare.

Coming to the studio for a treatment is about the whole experience: time for yourself to relax and recharge. With high quality, natural and organic skincare products, this is pure eco-luxe.

Bliss!

Daisy Green Skincare Studio, Deal

Follow on Instagram and Facebook!

Rest & Reset

"How beautiful it is to do nothing, and then rest afterward."
Spanish Proverb

It is vital for us to carve out time to rest and reset.

You might choose to ensure that your Sundays are the day to relax or it might be another day or time that suits your weekly routine. Keep some time sacred and this 'luxury' will pay dividends when you return to your busy life with increased vitality and creativity.

Experts agree that, in cold winter months when we are exposed to less natural light, we are more likely to need more rest and sleep. You may have heard our body clock referred to as our 'circadian rhythm' and the reduced daylight hours sends a clear signal to our body to prepare for sleep.

Living in such relentlessly hectic times, we should learn to rest without guilt or the need to justify to others!

Going Solo

"Solitude is enjoyed only when one is at peace with oneself."
Chinese Proverb

If you are someone who is uncomfortable with being alone, take yourself out of your comfort zone once in a while.

Try sitting in a cafe alone and once this feels more natural, you could try eating out or going to the cinema alone. Choosing to 'go solo' does not mean you will be lonely and gives you a chance to befriend yourself and gain focus in your life.

Yes, many of us are social animals and thrive in the company of others but it wouldn't hurt to experiment with some time for going it alone. You never know what you might discover.

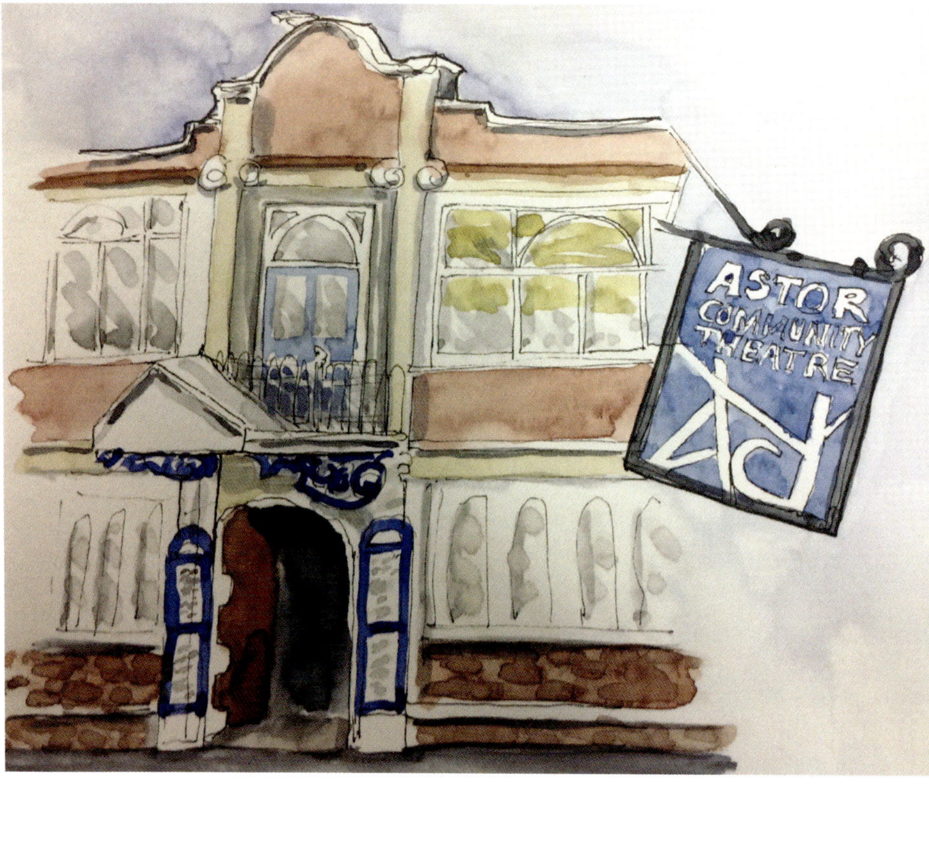
ASTOR
COMMUNITY
THEATRE

Try Something New

Having a go at something new could ignite a new passion, uncover a unique talent, connect you to a new relationship or spark a career change.

Here are a few fantastic reasons why you might like to engage in a new thing:

You may overcome fear, stimulate your creativity, get to know yourself, add skills to your set and potentially jolt yourself toward reinvigorating your life.

The Astor Community Theatre is in the heart of Deal, Kent and it has an inviting a tag line: something for everyone! Why not take a look at how you can get involved?

The Astor Community Theatre
Stanhope Road, Deal Kent

www.theastor.co.uk

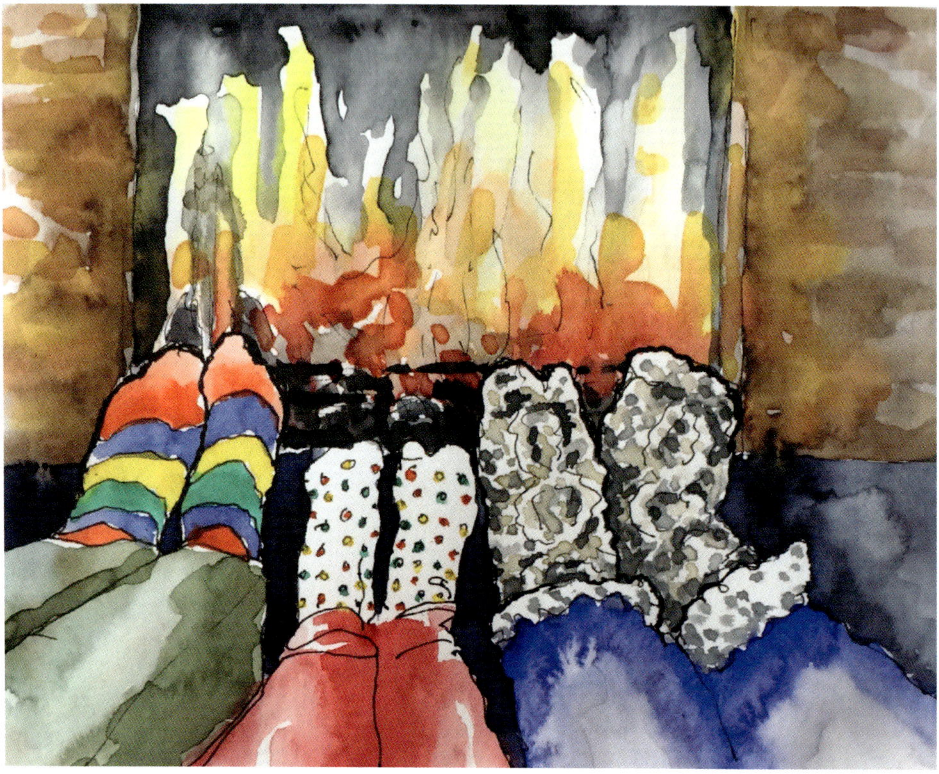

Relight Your Fire

It is hard to think of a more soul-nourishing experience than watching the hypnotic dance of flames from an open fire.

Our ancestors relied upon fire for warmth, light, cooking, protection and hunting. Gathering around a fire also provided social cohesion and relaxation (recent scientific studies have reported that sitting by a fire decreases blood pressure).

If your home is without a hearth, seek to create magical campfire moments during the summer months! To really complete the experience, tell stories across the crackling firelight, toast marshmallows and make sure at least one person gets their acoustic guitar out!

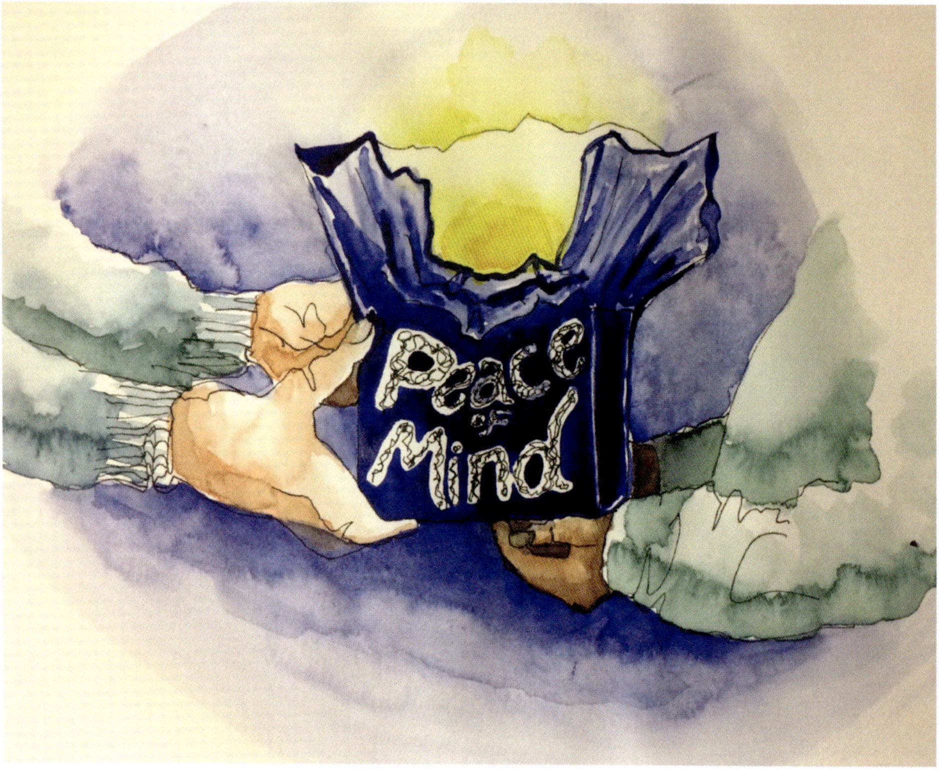
Peace of Mind

You Are Not Alone

Mental health problems affect around one in four people in any given year. These range from common problems such as depression and anxiety, to rarer problems such as schizophrenia and bipolar disorder.

Mind are a mental health charity providing somewhere to turn for advice and support if you are struggling with your mental health.

South Kent Mind covers Deal, Dover, Folkestone & Hythe.

"I can't thank South Kent Mind enough for their support."
South Kent Mind Member

South Kent Mind

Opening Hours:
9:30am - 3pm weekdays

www.southkentmind.org.uk

Your Body Is A Temple

"A man too busy to take care of his health is like a mechanic too busy to take care of his tools."
Spanish Proverb

If you are someone who struggles with the idea of denying yourself the 'naughty but nice', then you are not alone. A much more positive approach is to focus on what you CAN enjoy and gently guide yourself in that direction.

If you can drink plenty of water, take regular (enjoyable) exercise, eat more fruit and vegetables, improve your sleep pattern and sprinkle lots of laughter into your life then you are on the right track!

We all know the basic principles of a healthy lifestyle but having them written here may just nudge you to go and drink that glass of water or book that fitness class! It may inspire you to cook a delicious vegetarian meal or get out in the fresh air for that walk!

If you have a nagging feeling about ANYTHING health-related, don't delay in contacting a Health Professional.

Risk it for a Biscuit

"You have to take risks. We will only understand the miracle of life fully when we allow the unexpected to happen."
Paulo Coelho

Taking risks is challenging for many but the benefits of being a bit more of a chancer are numerous.

Reading this, you might have your own clear idea of what a 'risk' is to you. Is it jumping out of an aeroplane for a skydive or is it asking for that promotion at work? Perhaps, it is approaching that handsome man you see at the train station every day or simply speaking out about an injustice.

If you take a risk, you may discover an opportunity, develop a new skill, feel more 'alive' and engaged. The sense of accomplishment after taking a risk can be immense and really develop confidence and resilience.

You are not a passive observer of life but an active participant. Don't wait in the wings!

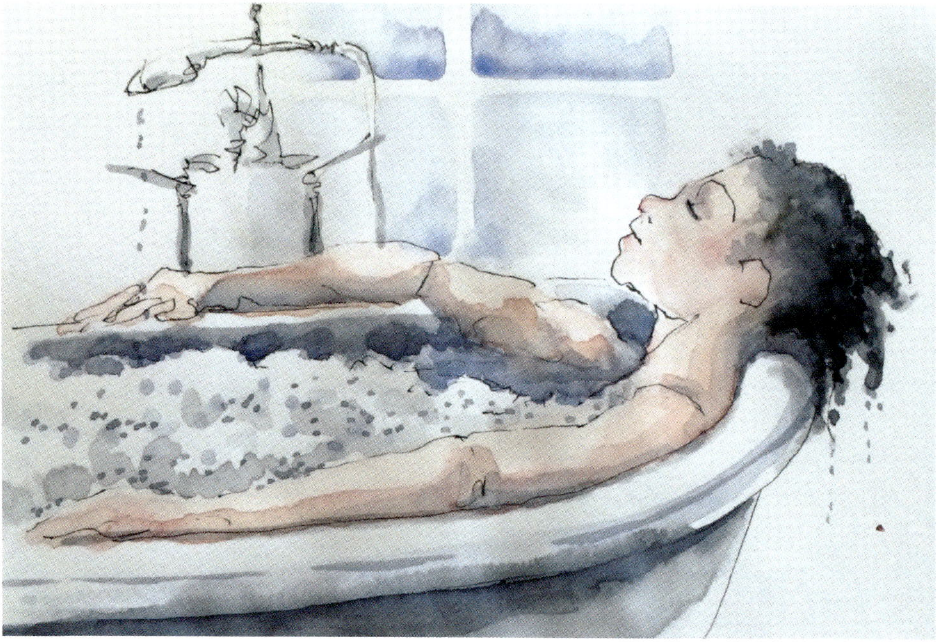

Soak It Up

Relaxing in a hot bath is a powerful and widely available (!) treat for the senses, particularly in the winter months.

Hot baths have been proven to aid sleep, relieve muscle tension, improve circulation, ease anxiety and even lower blood sugar levels!

Make sacred time in your evening to light candles, pour yourself a glass of something and maybe listen to your favourite soothing music.

Give your body the respect, nurturing and love it deserves and craves.

Be Flexible

"The bamboo that bends is stronger than the oak that resists."
Japanese Proverb

In recent times, life has required us to be flexible.

We can be flexible in body but also in mind: Flexibility in the body can provide relaxation and an improvement in strength, posture and balance. It is likely to contribute to a positive state of mind and increased confidence. Yoga and Pilates are a great place to start!

Mental flexibility is more about keeping an agile mind by our ability to adapt and live a more creative, resilient life by learning to 'roll with the punches' we are faced with.

Let me see you flex!

Give Gifts Generously

This doesn't mean you need to spend lots of money!

You could make homemade jam or biscuits or perhaps re-gift something you already have at home (such as an unused candle or new bath products).*

If you have just read a life-changing book, why not pass it on to a friend or family member who will also enjoy it?*

You might gift someone your time and advice.

It really is the thought that counts.

*these are also handy ways of regularly decluttering, recycling and simplifying! Everyone's a winner!

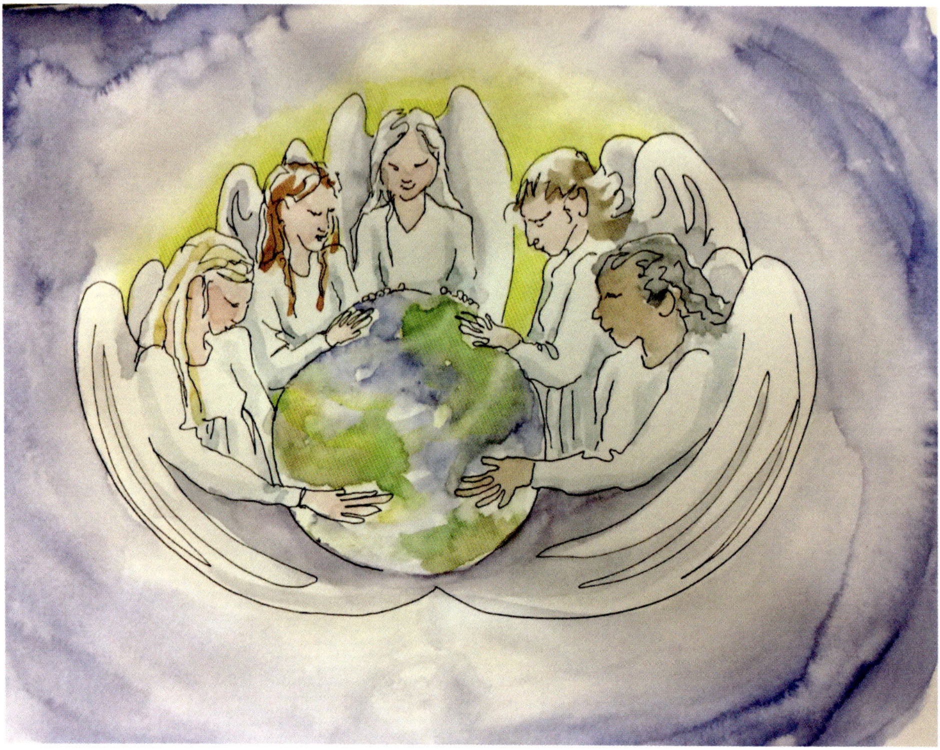

Seek Guidance

There are a handful of times in our lives where we may reach an agonising crossroads and we do not know which path to take. Many of us have been there.

During these times, we may turn to spiritual guidance to bring clarity and decisiveness to our impasse.

Hannah Macintyre is a clairvoyant medium working internationally but based in Kent, UK. She works with a talented team of handpicked mediums to offer a variety of different readings. Her journey with spirituality has been profound and life changing and it is her mission to spread messages of love and hope from the other side.

For further information, take a look at www.readingsandreiki.co.uk.

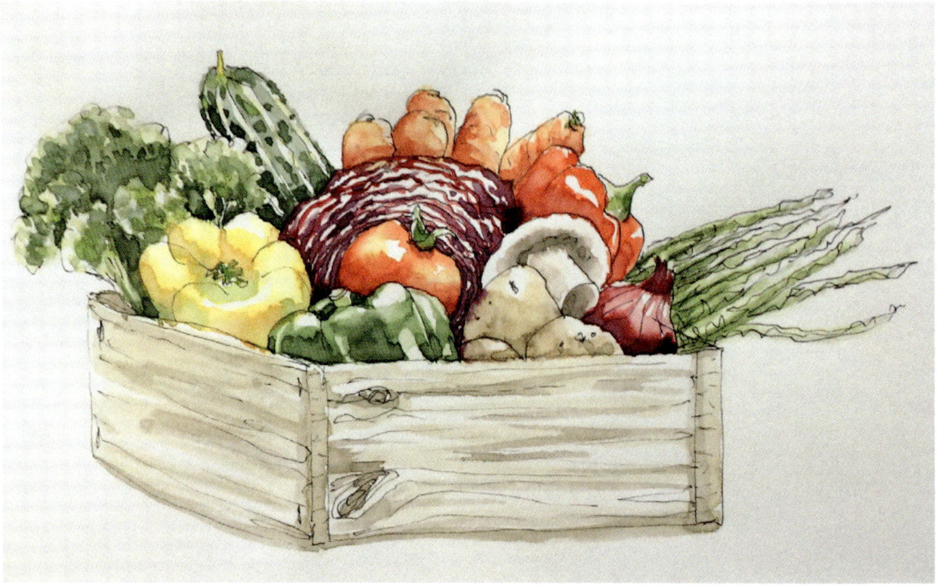

Veg Out

Consuming plenty of fresh fruit and vegetables is a sure way to feel on top form.

Eating local and seasonal produce is environmentally friendly because it involves less transportation and storage.

The nutritional value of harvested ingredients that arrive on your plate faster (without travelling halfway around the world first) is far higher because food stored for long periods of time have a decline in antioxidants such as Vitamin C. If you eat food grown in local soil, you can usually taste the difference!

By buying locally, you are also supporting your local farmers and the local economy.

Go on... veg out!

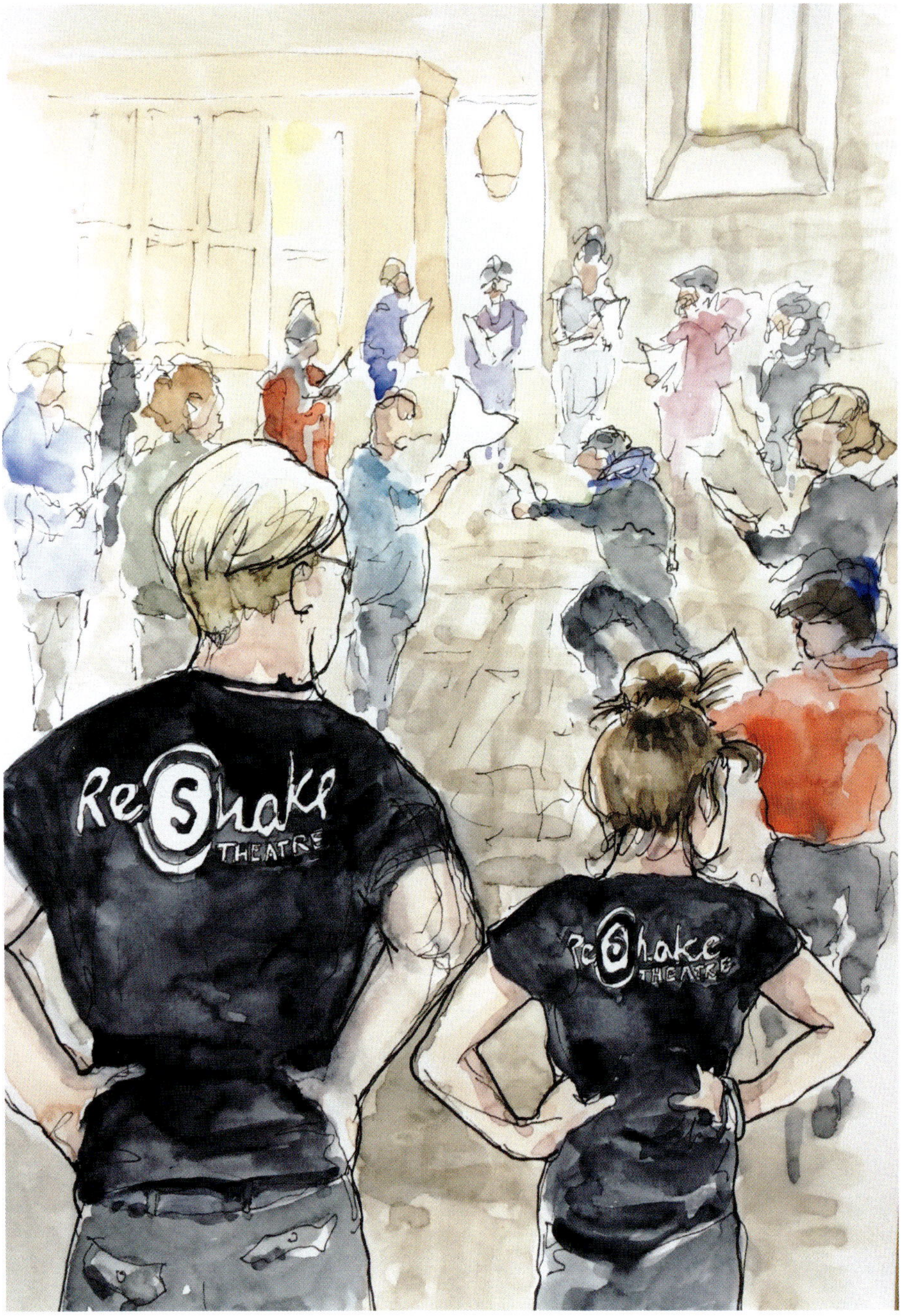
ReShake
THEATRE
ReShake
THEATRE

Switch The Script!

"All the world's a stage, and all the men and women merely players."
Shakespeare

We are free to play many roles in this lifetime and enter and exit various scenes and acts. This famous phrase from As You Like It refers to the world being like a stage show with humans coming and going like characters in a play.

Think of your life like a play and don't be afraid to throw in a plot twist every now and again! People come and go in and out of our lives and this is both natural and healthy. Are you suffering from stage fright? Have you been typecast? Are you avoiding the subtext? Are you the protagonist in your own story?

ReShake Theatre are the company-in-residence at St Mary's Arts Centre in the medieval town of Sandwich, Kent who specialise in bringing new life to old plays. They are committed to bringing free and affordable professional theatre training to the local community via Masterclasses in Shakespeare and have links with The Rose Playhouse and The Marlowe Society.

For further information, follow them on Facebook!

St Mary's Arts Centre is a stunning 14th century building and unique Arts & Events Venue.

Strand Street, Sandwich, Kent.

www.stmarysartscentre.org.uk

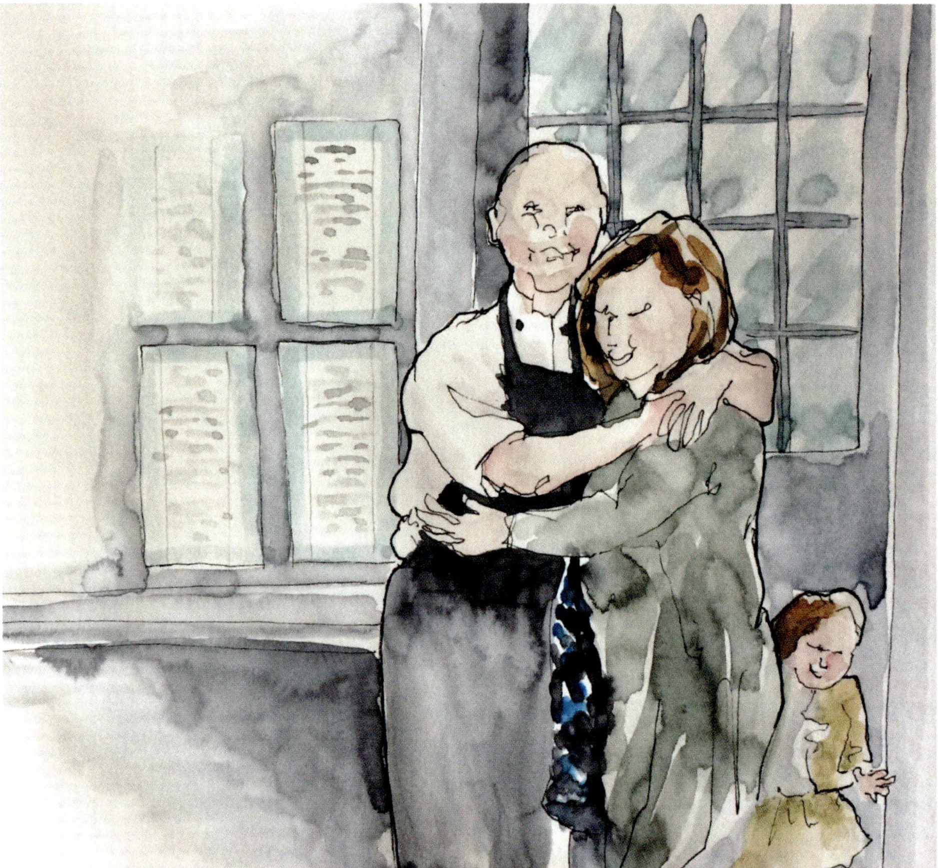

In The Club!

Tasting delicious food inspired by famous chefs and culinary delights from around the world can almost make you feel like you're on holiday in your own town!

The Dining Club is owned and run by husband-and-wife team, Scott & Suzanne Roberts who can also offer bespoke catering for special events such as weddings and birthdays. There is something really personal about being greeted and seated by Suzanne, whilst her husband, Scott, is cooking up a storm in the kitchen!

The unique qualities of this fine restaurant in Deal also include a more private dining experience in one of the beautifully decorated Georgian rooms. The joy of a mouth-watering set menu means less time wasted deciding and ordering on the day and more quality, uninterrupted time spent with your company!

You can bring your own drink to The Dining Club which keeps the cost of a leisurely multi-course meal surprisingly affordable!

The Dining Club
69 Middle Street
Deal
Kent

www.thediningclubdeal.co.uk

Plan for the Future

Who doesn't love a list?

It has been proven that writing down your goals can help you ensure they actually happen!

List a few things you are hoping to achieve next year.

Is it…

Going on a dream holiday?

Improving your fitness?

Studying?

Finding the love of your life?

Eating a more balanced diet?

Writing a novel?

Whatever it is, writing it down and considering the 'how' will undoubtedly assist you.

Another good technique is announcing your intentions to others!

Take Stock

As the year draws to a close, reflect on the many achievements you have made. This could be a good time to make adjustments to life goals and consider plans for the new year.

No doubt there will have been losses and gains but you will have learned from these experiences in equal measure.

Take time to feel gratitude for the many positives in your life and do not dwell on anything that didn't quite go as planned.

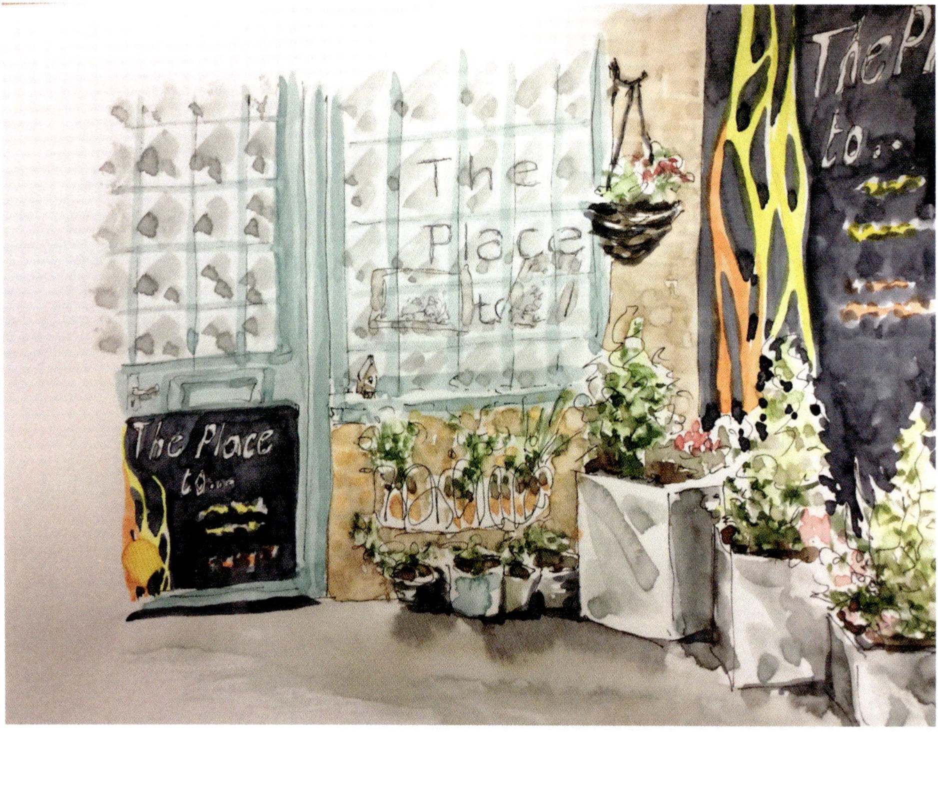
The Place to
The Place to...
The P
to..

The Place To....Be

Whether we like it or not, it is difficult to avoid the consumerism of Christmas.

Whilst you are out and about shopping for gifts, be mindful of supporting local businesses where possible.

Can you buy someone a unique piece of artwork or a handmade bobble hat? How about quirky bookends or stylish plant pots?

Buying a unique gift is not only thoughtful and special, it may really boost the livelihood of your local crafts people.

Over the years, Zenia & Steve Ford met so many talented people of all ages. The diverse skill of these people in crafting, drawing, writing and making inspired the idea of creating an affordable, rentable space in which their unique creations could be sold.

The Place To
1c George Alley, Deal

www.theplaceto.co.uk
Or follow on Instagram or Facebook!

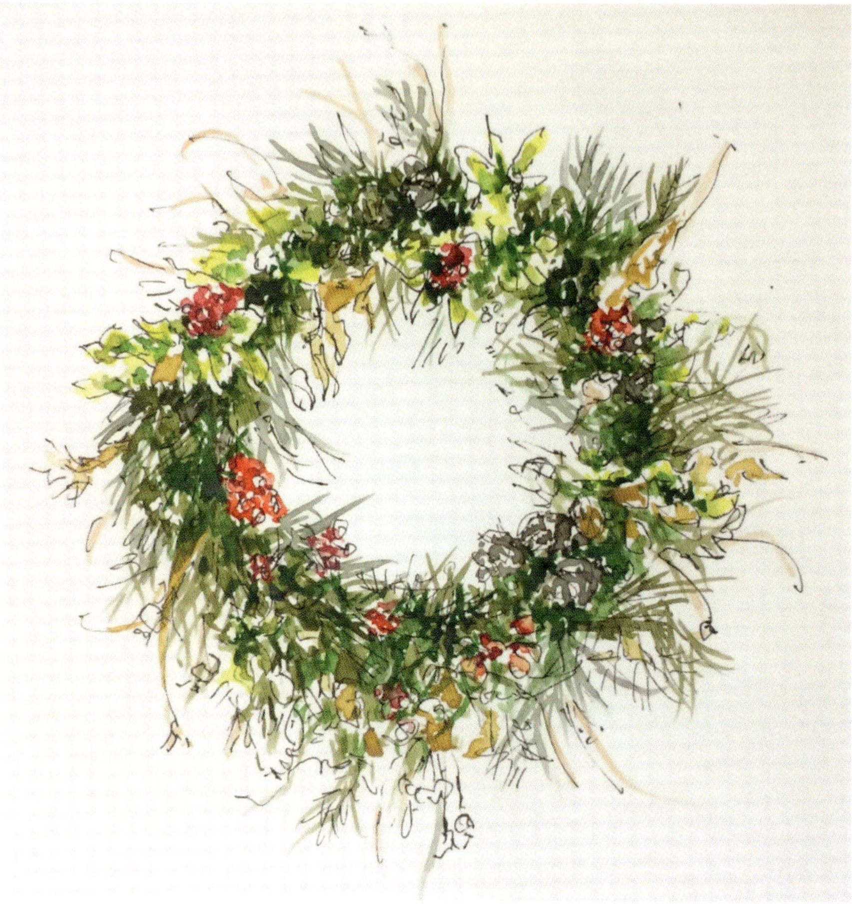

Get Festive

According to Christians, we hang wreaths on our doors at Christmas time to represent the crown of thorns worn on the cross and by using evergreen branches we signify eternal life. Hanging a wreath on your door is a way of inviting the spirit of Christ into your home.

However, some believe the tradition originated in Ancient Rome where wreaths were hung on doors to represent victory. German folklore is also another popular theory where the wreath is seen to represent sustainability in the bleak winter months.

Whatever your belief, we can all agree that hanging a beautiful wreath on your door creates a sense of pride and enthusiasm for the festive season.

Laura Tricker is a designer, obsessed with all things Deal.

With a background in textile design for the fashion industry, Tormore School House was born out of a desire to celebrate creative living by the coast.

Forever inspired by Deal's surrounding nature and all the beauty within, Laura works to create natural and thoughtful pieces for you and your home by the sea, including seasonal wreaths.

Browse her shop at www.tormoreschoolhouse.com

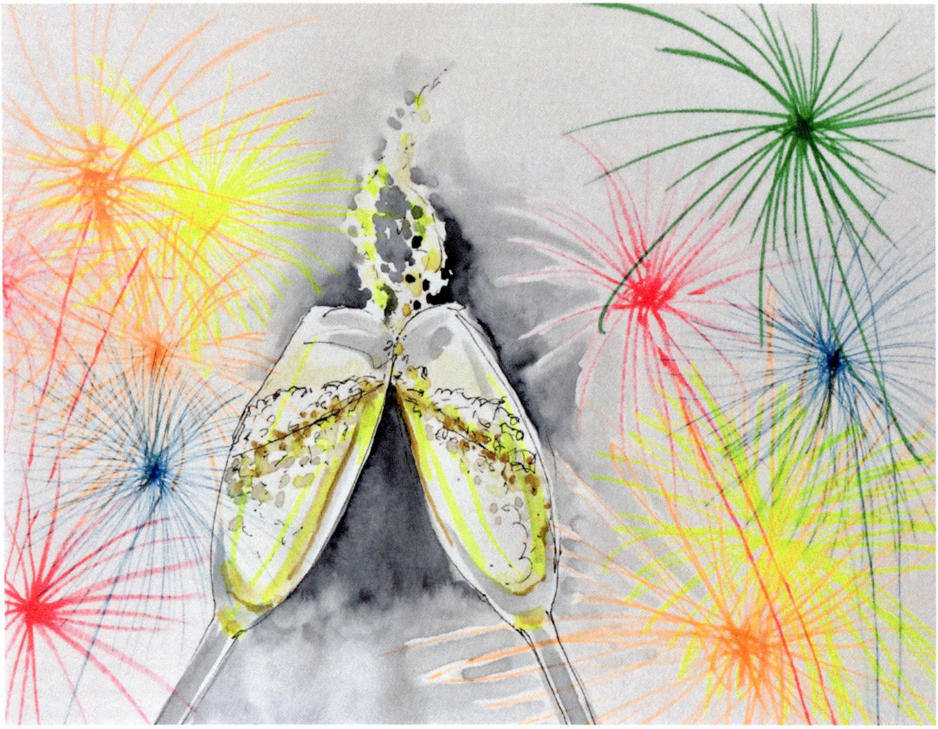

Celebrate

"The more you celebrate your life, the more there is to celebrate."
Oprah Winfrey

As the year comes to a close, toast to how far you have travelled on your journey and how you have tackled any obstacles on the way.

It is common for people to celebrate 'big things' in life such as milestone birthdays, births, marriages and a promotion or new job but reward yourself by celebrating far more regularly.

Each evening, before you go to sleep, remind yourself of the positive achievements of that day and disregard anything negative.

Be kind to yourself. You are worth celebrating.

Lizzie Willis

With a childhood jam-packed with noisy siblings, live music, laughter, beach days, woodland adventures, jumble sales and love, I 'grew up' in Deal, Kent, UK.

My career includes a large helping of Performing Arts, several big dollops of teaching and learning and some sprinkles of creative event planning. I am usually cooking up a few creative ideas simultaneously and I fully intend to squeeze the most out of my time here on Planet Earth.

I currently live a heart-centred life in my hometown of Deal with my two awesome sons.

Angela Malone

Born in the bustle of Brooklyn, New York but raised on the golden sands of Margate beach, I always knew I was an artist. The eldest of six children, mother of two and a grandmother to five, I've scarcely had time to stop and smell any roses!

But I did manage to gain a BA in my 50's, study for my MA in my 60's and am looking forward to exciting times in my 70's! I've packed in exhibitions in France, Germany, Vienna and the British Museum so far and even won some International prizes, so my motto (and advice) is 'just say yes' and then figure out how it will work afterwards, it isn't always obvious but it usually turns out fine.

Special Thanks To:

Elisa Ellis Fitness

Hut 55 & Garage Coffee

Deal Hypnotherapy

Purpledaisy LTD

Your Little Green Shop

Jenkinson Estates

Felderland Farm

The Coastguard

Dave Willis Tai Chi

Sandwich Accounts

Funky Monks

Mike's Bikes

81 Beach Street

The History Project

Lisa Taylor Designs

The Rose

Dickinson & Son

Urban Chic

DON'T WALK WALK Gallery

The Lighthouse

Deal Rental Bureau

Angela Malone Art

Deal Radio

Daisy Green Skincare Studio

Hannah Macintyre – Readings & Reiki

The Dining Club

The Hayman's Kitchen

The Place To...

Tormore School House

This book is also proud to support:

Sandwich Bird Observatory

Deal Area Foodbank

The Astor Community Theatre

South Kent Mind

ReShake Theatre

Kensei Taiko